The Last Abbot
Of
Glastonbury
And His Companions:
An Historical Sketch

by

Francis Aidan Gasquet, D.D., O.S.B.

St Athanasius Press

ISBN: 9798645690526

St Athanasius Press
www.stathanasiuspress.com
melwaller@gmail.com

(email is the best way to reach us)

CONTENTS

Chapter I   4
Glastonbury

Chapter II   12
Richard Whiting

Chapter III   23
Richard Whiting elected Abbot

Chapter IV   31
Troubles in Church and State

Chapter V   42
Richard Whiting as Abbot of Glastonbury

Chapter VI   58
The Beginning of the End

Chapter VII   73
The Martyrdom

Chapter VIII   83
Abbot Hugh Cook of Reading

Chapter IX   107
The Last Abbot of Colchester

Chapter I

Glastonbury

The prospect from the Roman camp of Masbury, on the Mendip hills of Somerset, is one to be remembered. The country presents itself to the view as in a map. In front a vast plain stretches out into the dim blue horizon across Dorsetshire to the shores of the English Channel. To the east the hills fall and rise like the swell of the sea in a series of vales and heights till they are lost in the distance. Westward the landscape is more varied, the ground, which at the spectator's feet had attained well-nigh to the dignity of a mountain, sinks away in a succession of terraces to the level country lying between it and the waters of the Severn sea. From the midst of this plain there rises clear and sharp against the sky, like a pyramid, a hill crowned with a tower, which forms from all points the most marked feature of the scene. Neither the glancing of the sunlight from the surface of the sea some fifteen miles away, nor the glimpse that is caught between the trees of the gray towers and gables of the great cathedral church of Welk, nor yet the sight of the spire of Doulting, calling up as it does, memories of Saint Aldhelm, can long restrain the eye from turning once again to gaze on the conical hill with its tower which stands out in the landscape. Remarkable alike in its contour and in its situation, these do not constitute its chief attraction, for it speaks not only to the eye but to the mind also; it is Nature's monument marking a spot of more than ordinary interest. The shadows of tradition seem still to hover over the hill and recall a past which is lost in the dimness of legend. More than all, however, the last record which marks the place in the pages of history brings to mind a deed of desecration and of blood perpetrated in the evil days which brought ruin to the most famous sanctuary on English soil, for here suffered for conscience sake Richard Whiting, last abbot of the far-famed abbey of Glastonbury which nestled at its foot, thus making a worthy close to a history without parallel in the annals of our country.

The history of Glastonbury is the history of its abbey; without its abbey Glastonbury were nothing. Even among those great ecclesiastical institutions, the Benedictine abbeys of mediaeval England, the history of Glastonbury has a character all its own. I will not insult its venerable age, says a recent historian, by so much as contrasting it with the foundations of yesterday which arose under the influence of the Cistercian movement, for they play but a small part indeed in the history of this church and realm, Glastonbury is something more than Netley and Tintern, Rievaux and Fountains. It is something more again than the Benedictine houses which arose at the bidding of the Norman Conqueror, of his race and of his companions; more than Selby and Battle, and Shrewsbury and Reading. It is in its own special aspect something more even than the royal minster of Saint Peter, the crowning place of Harold and of William, which came to supplant Glastonbury as the burial place of kings. Nay, it stands out distinct even among the great and venerable foundations of English birth which were already great and venerable when this country fell into the hands of the Norman. There is something in Glastonbury which one looks for in vain at Peterborough and Crowland and Evesham, or even at Winchester and Canterbury; all these are the works of our own, our English people; they go back to the days of our ancient kingship, they go back – some of them – even to the days when Augustine preached, and Theodore fixed the organisation of the growing English Church; but they go back no further. We know their beginnings, we know their founders; their history, nay, their very legends do not dare to trace up their foundations beyond the time of the coming of Saxon and Angle into this island. At Glastonbury, and at Glastonbury alone, we instinctively feel that the name of England is not all, for here, and here alone, we walk with easy steps, with no thought of any impassable barrier, from the realm of Saxon Ina back to that of Arthur, the hero king of the British race. Alongside of the memory and the tombs of the West-Saxon princes, who broke the power of the Northmen, there still abides the memory of the British prince who checked for a generation the advance of the Saxon.

But at Glastonbury even this is a small matter. The legends of the spot go back to the very days of the Apostles. Here, and here alone on English soil, we are linked, not only to the beginnings of English Christianity, but to the beginnings of Christianity itself We are met at the outset by the tradition that the spot was made sacred as the dwelling of a multitude of the just, and its soil hallowed by the bodies of numerous saints, "whose souls now rejoice," says an ancient writer, "in the possession of God in heaven." For here were believed to have found a resting place the twelve disciples of Philip the Apostle, sent by him to Britain, under the leadership of Joseph of Arimathea, who had buried our Lord. "We know not," continues our author in his simple style, "whether they really repose here, although we have read that they sojourned in the place for nine years; but here dwelt assuredly many of their disciples, ever twelve in number, who in imitation of them led a hermit's life until unto them came Saint Patrick, the great Apostle of the Irish and first abbot of the hallowed spot. Here, too, rests Saint Benen, the disciple of Saint Patrick; here Saint Gildas, the historian of the British; here Saint David, bishop of Menevia, and here the holy hermit Indractus with his seven companions, all sprung from the royal race. Here rest the relics of a band of holy Irish pilgrims, who returning from a visit to the shrines of Rome, turned aside to Glastonbury out of love to Saint Patrick's memory and were martyred in a village named Shapwick.

Hither, not long after, their remains were brought by Ina, our glorious king."

Such stories of the mediaeval scribe, however little worthy of credit in point of detail, represent, there can be little doubt, a substantial truth. For as in later centuries there were brought hither even from far distant Northumbria the relics of Paulinus, and Aidan and Ceolfrid, of Boisil, of Benet Biscop and of others for security on the advance of the Danes, so too in earlier dangers there were carried to Glastonbury, to save them from the blind fury of the pagan Saxon, all that was most sacred and venerated in the churches of Christian Britain,

"No fiction, no dream could have dared," writes the historian, "to set down the names of so many worthies of the earlier races of the British Islands in the Liber Vitae of Durham or of Peterborough. Now I do not ask you to believe these legends; I do ask you to believe that there was some special cause why legends of this kind should grow in such a shape, and in such abundance round Glastonbury alone of all the great monastic churches of Britain."
Though these Glastonbury legends need not be believed as the record of facts, still it has been well said that "the very existence of those legends is a very great fact." The simple truth is that the remoteness and isolation of Glastonbury preserved it from attack, until Christianity had won its way among

the West Saxons. So that when at last the Teutonic
conqueror came to Avalon, he had already bowed his
head to the cross and been washed in the waters of
Christian baptism. His coming was thus not to de-
stroy, but to give renewed life to the already ancient
monastic sanctuary, The sacred precincts, hitherto
held by Britons only, now received monks of English race some time before King Ina, its new founder, following the example of his father, Caedwalla,
after a reign of seven and thirty years, resigned his
crown, to journey to Rome, desiring to end his pilgrimage on earth in the near neighbourhood of the
holy places, so that he might the more readily be
received by the saints themselves into the celestial
kingdom.

And when later the Danes overwhelmed the land, it
was this hallowed spot that was destined to be the
centre from which not merely a vigorous monastic revival spread throughout England, but whence
the kingdom itself was raised by a great reformer
to a new pitch of secular greatness; for it was here
that Dunstan as a boy, brought by his father on a
pilgrimage to the churches of Saint Mary and Saint
Peter the Apostle, "built of olden time," passed the
night in prayer. Overcome by sleep the boy saw in
a dream an aged man, clothed in snowy vesture,
leading him, not through the simple chapels and
half – ruined buildings which then occupied the
site, but through the fair alleys of a spacious church

and comely claustral buildings, whilst he told him
that thus was Glastonbury to be rebuilt by him, and
that he was to be its future head. This, though but a
dream, was yet a dream which must have been re-
lated by Dunstan himself in after years. The young
day-dreams of a strong nature have a , tendency to
realise themselves in later life, and this boyish vi-
sion of a renovated Glastonbury, the outward sign
of a new monastic spirit, manifests the workings of
a mind influenced, but prepared to be influenced, by
the past memories and the present decay of the holy
place. Nor did these early images pass away in view
of the brilliant prospects that opened out before the
young cleric, who had all the advantages of personal
capacity and powerful connections, and so he betook
himself to remote and solitary Glastonbury, to work
out the realization of his monastic ideals. Dunstan
built up its walls with the essentially practical end
of securing the primary requirements of monastic
enclosure, and the buildings were just like those he
dreamed of in his boyhood. He threw on his brother
Wulfric the entire temporal business and management of the estates, so that he, freed from the en-
cumbrance of all external affairs, might build up the
souls of those who had committed themselves to his
direction. It was here at Glastonbury, under the care
of Saint Dunstan, that Saint Ethelwold was formed
and fashioned to be the chief instrument in carrying
out his monastic policy. Here, too, Saint Elphege the
martyr, and a successor of Dunstan on the throne of

Canterbury lived his monastic life. And from Avalon, too, about the same time, went forth the monk Sigfrid, as the evangelist of pagan Norway.

With such a history, such legends of the past and such a renewal as the firm and lofty spirit of Dunstan effected in its refoundation, it is no wonder that the repute of Glastonbury drew to it a crowd of fervent monks and the ample benefactions of devout and faithful friends, so that from henceforward there was no monastic house in England which for splendour or wealth could compare with this ancient sanctuary. Through the later Middle Ages, to the people of England Glastonbury was a Roma secunda. Strangers came from afar to visit the holy ground, and pilgrim rests marked the roads which led to it. Foreigners coming in ships which brought their freight to the great port of Bristol, hardly ever failed to turn aside to visit this home of the saints, whilst memorials of the sanctuary were carried by the Bristol merchants into foreign lands.

Even now, as it lies in ruin, the imagination can conceive the wonder with which a stranger, on reaching the summit of the hill, still known as the Pilgrims Way^ saw spread out before him Glastonbury Abbey in all its vast extent, with its towers and chapels, its broad courts and cloisters, crowned with the mighty church, the fitting shrine of the sacred relics and holy memories which had brought him thither.

Chapter II

Richard Whiting

Never, perhaps, was Glastonbury in greater glory than at the moment when Richard Whiting was elected to rule the house as abbot.

Richard Whiting was born probably in the early years of the second half of the fifteenth century. The civil war between the Houses of York and Lancaster was then at its height, and his boyhood must have been passed amid the popular excitement of the Wars of the Roses and the varied fortunes of King Edward IV. It is not unimportant to bear this in mind, since the personal experience in his youth of the troubles and dangers of civil strife can hardly have failed to impress their obvious lesson strongly upon his mind, and to influence him when the willfulness of Henry brought the country to the very verge of' civil war, with its attendant miseries and horrors.

The abbot's family was west-country in its origin and was connected distantly with that of Bishop Stapeldon, of Exeter, the generous founder of Exeter College, Oxford. Its principal member was possessed of considerable estates in Devon and Somerset, but Richard Whiting came of a younger branch of the family, numbered among the tenant holders

of Glastonbury possessions in the fertile valley of
Warington. The name is found in the annals of other
religious houses. About the time of Richard Whiting's birth, for example, another Richard, probably
an uncle, was camerarius, or chamberlain, in the
monastery of Bath, an office which in after years, at
the time of his election as abbot, the second Richard
held in the Abbey of Glastonbury. Many years later,
at the beginning of the troubles which involved the
religious houses in the reign of Henry VIII, a Jane
Whiting, daughter of John, probably a near relative
of the Abbot of Glastonbury "was shorn and had
taken the habit as a nun in the convent of Wilton;"
whilst later still, when new foundations of English
religious life were being laid in foreign countries,
two of Abbot Whiting's nieces became postulants for
the veil in the English Franciscan house at Bruges.

Nothing is known for certain about the childhood
and youth of Richard Whiting; but it may be safely
conjectured that he received his early education
and training within the walls of his future monastic
home. The antiquary Hearne says that "the monks
of Glastonbury kept a free school, where poor men's
sons were bred up as well as gentlemen's and were
fitted for the universities." And some curious legal
proceedings, which involved an enquiry as to the
Carthusian martyr, blessed Richard Bere, reveal the
fact that as a boy he had been "brought up at the
charges of his uncle," Abbot Bere, in the Glaston-

bury school. The pleadings show that Richard Bere was probably the son of one of the tenants of the abbey lands, and among those who testify to the fact of his having been a boy in the school were "Nicholas Roe, of Glastonbury, gent," and "John Fox, of Glastonbury, yeoman," both of whom had been his fellow scholars "in the said abbey together," and Thomas Penny, formerly Abbot Bere's servant, who spoke to the nephew Richard as having been in the school at the monastery, whence as he remembered he afterwards proceeded to Oxford. What is thus known, almost by accident, about the early education of the martyred Carthusian, may with fair certainty be inferred in the case of Richard Whiting. The boy's training in the claustral school was succeeded by the discipline of the monastic novitiate: and it was doubtless in early youth, as was then the custom, that he joined the community of the great Benedictine monastery of the west country.

Glastonbury, with its long, unbroken history, had had its days of prosperity and its days of trouble, its periods of laxity and days of recovery, and when Whiting first took the monastic habit report did not speak too well of the state of the establishment. John Selwood, the abbot, had held the office since 1457, and under his rule, owing, probably in some measure at least, to the demoralising influence of the constant civil commotions, discipline grew slack and the good name of the abbey had suffered. But it would seem that, as is so often the case, rumour with its many tongues had exaggerated the disorders, since after a careful examination carried out under Bishop Stillington's orders by four ecclesiastics unconnected with the diocese, no stringent injunctions were apparently imposed, and Abbot Selwood continued to rule the house for another twenty years.

From Glastonbury, Whiting was sent to Cambridge to complete his education, and his name appears amongst those who took their M. A. degree in 1483. About the same time the register of the university records the well-known names of Richard Reynolds, the Bridgettine priest of Sion, of John Houghton and William Exmew, both Carthusians, and all three afterwards noble martyrs in the cause of Catholic unity, for which Whiting was also later called upon to sacrifice his life. The blessed John Fisher also, although no longer a student, still remained in close connection with the university, when Richard Whiting came up from Glastonbury to Cambridge.

After taking his degree the young Benedictine monk returned to his monastery, and there probably would have been occupied in teaching stay at the university in preparation for his degree in Arts, would have specially qualified him, and in all probability he was thus engaged till his ordination to the priesthood, some fifteen years later. During this period one or two events of importance to the monks of the abbey may be briefly noted.

In 1493, John Selwood, who had been abbot for thirty-six years, died. The monks having obtained the King's leave to proceed with the election of a successor,^ met for the purpose, and made their choice, without apparently having previously obtained the usual approval of the bishop of the diocese. This neglect was caused possibly by their ignorance of the forms of procedure, as so long a time had intervened since the last election. It may be also that in the long continued absence of the Bishop of Bath and Wells from his See they overlooked this form. Be this as it may, Bishop Fox, then the occupant of the See, on hearing of the election of John Wasyn without his approval, applied to the king for permission to cancel the election. This having been granted, he successfully claimed the right to nominate to the office, and on 20th January, 1494, by his commissary. Dr. Richard Nicke, Canon of Wells, and afterwards Bishop of Norwich, he installed Richard Bere in the abbatial chair of Glastonbury.

In the fourth year of this abbot's rule, Somerset and the neighbourhood of Glastonbury was disturbed by the passage of armed men – insurgents against the authority of King Henry VII and the royal troops sent against them – which must have sadly broken in upon the quiet of the monastic life. In the early summer of 1497 the Cornish rebels who had risen in resistance to the heavy taxation of Henry, passed through Glastonbury and Wells on their way to London. Their number was estimated at from six to fifteen thousand, and the country for miles around was at night lighted up by their camp fires. Their poverty was dire, their need most urgent, and although it is recorded that no act of violence or pillage was perpetrated by this undisciplined band, still their support was a burden on the religious houses and the people of the districts through which they passed.

Hardly had this rising been suppressed than Somerset was again involved in civil commotions. Early in the autumn of 1497 Perkin Warbeck assembled his rabble forces – "howbeit, they were poor and naked" – round Taunton, and on the 21st September the advanced guard of the king's army arrived at Glastonbury, and was sheltered in the monastery and its dependencies. The same night the adventurer fled to sanctuary, leaving his 8,000 followers to their own devices; and on the 29th of this same month Henry himself reached Bath and moved forward at once to join his other forces at Wells and Glastonbury. With him came Bishop Oliver King, who, although he had held the See of Bath and Wells for three years, had never yet visited his cathedral city, and who now hurried on before his royal master to be enthroned as bishop a few hours before he in that capacity took part in the reception of the king. Henry had with him some 30,000 men, when on

Saint Jerome's day he entered Wells, and took up his lodgings with Dr. Cunthorpe in the deanery. The following day, Sunday, 1 October, was spent at Wells, where the king attended in the Cathedral at a solemn Te Deum in thanksgiving for his bloodless victory. Early on the Monday he passed on to Glastonbury, and was lodged by Abbot Bere within the precincts of the monastery.

The abbey was then at the height of its glory, for Bere was in every way fitted for the position to which the choice of Fox had elevated him. A witness in the trial spoken of above describes Abbot Bere as " a grave, wise and discreet man, just and upright in all his ways, and for so accounted of almost all sorts of people." Another deposes that he "was good, honest, virtuous, wise and discreet, as well as a grave man, and for those virtues esteemed in as great reputation as few of his coat and calling in England at that time were better accounted of." On the interior discipline and the exterior administration of his house alike he bestowed a watchful care, and under his prudent administration the monastic buildings and church received many useful and costly additions. At great expense he built the suite of rooms afterwards known as "the King's lodgings," and added more than one chapel to the time-honoured sanctuary of Glastonbury. At the west end of the town he built the Church of Saint Benen, now commonly known as Saint Benedict's, which

bears in every portion of the structure his rebus. His
care for the poor was manifested by the almshouses
he established, and the thought he bestowed on the
prudent ordering of the lowly spital of Saint Marga-
ret's, Taunton. Beyond this, Bere was a learned man,
as well as a careful administrator, and even Erasmus submitted to his judgment. In a letter written a
few years after this abbot's death this great scholar
records how he had long known the reputation of
the Abbot of Glastonbury. His bosom friend, Richard Pace, the well-known ambassador of Wolsey in
many difficult negotiations, had told him how to Bere's liberality he owed his education and his success
in life to the abbot's judicious guidance. For this
reason, Erasmus, who had made a translation of the
sacred Scriptures from the Greek, which he thought
showed a "more polished style" than Saint Jerome's
version, submitted his work to the judgment of the
abbot. Bere opposed the publication, and Erasmus
bowed to the abbot's opinion, which in after years
he acknowledged as correct.^ Henry the Seventh,
who ever delighted in the company of learned men,
must have been pleased with the entertainment he
received at Glastonbury, where the whole cost was
borne by the abbot. It is possible, by reason of the
knowledge the king then derived of the great abili-
ties of Bere, that six years afterwards, in 1503, he
made choice of him to carry the congratulations of
England to Cardinal John Angelo de Medicis, when
he ascended the pontifical throne as Pius IV.

The troubles of Somerset did not end with the retirement of the royal troops. Though the country did not rise in support of the Cornish movement, it appears to have somewhat sympathised with it, and at Wells Lord Audley joined the insurgents as their leader. For this sympathy Henry made them pay; and the rebels' line of march can be traced by the record of the heavy fines levied upon those who had been supposed to have "aided and comforted" them. Sir Amyas Paulet – the first Paulet of Hinton Saint George – was one of the commissioners sent to exact this pecuniary punishment, and from his record it would appear that nearly all in Somerset were fined. The abbots of Ford and Cleeve, of Muchelney and Athelney, with others, had extended their charity to the starving insurgents, and Sir Amyas made them pay somewhat smartly for their pity. Somehow Glastonbury appears to have escaped the general penalty; probably the abbot's entertainment of the king saved the abbey, although some of the townsfolk did not escape the fine.^ This severe treatment must have had more than a passing effect. The generation living at the time of the suppression of the abbey could well remember the event. They knew well what was the meaning of the heavy hand of a king, and had felt at their own hearths what were the ravages of an army. This may go far to explain how it happened that in Somersetshire there was no Pilgrimage of Grace.

Meantime Richard Whiting had witnessed these
troubles, which came so near home, from the seclusion of the monastic enclosure in which he had
been preparing for the reception of sacred orders.
The Bishop of Bath and Wells, Oliver King, had
not remained in his diocese after the public reception of Henry. He was much engaged in the secular
affairs of the kingdom, and his episcopal functions
were relegated to the care of a suffragan, Thomas
Cornish, titular Bishop of Tinos, also at this time
Vicar of Saint Cuthberts, Wells, and Chancellor of
the Diocese. From the hands of this prelate Dom
Richard Whiting received the minor order of acolyte
in the month of September, 1498. In the two succeeding years he was made sub-deacon and deacon,
and on the 6th March, 1501, he was elevated to the
sacred order of the priesthood. The ordination was
held in Wells by Bishop Cornish in the chapel of the
Blessed Virgin, by the cathedral cloisters – a chapel
long since destroyed, and the foundations of which
have recently been discovered.

For the next five and twenty years we know very little about Richard Whiting. It is more than probable
that his life was passed entirely in the seclusion of
the cloister and in the exercise of the duties imposed
upon him by obedience. In 1505, the register of the
University of Cambridge shows that he returned
there, and took his final degree as Doctor in Theol-
ogy. In his monastery he held the office of "Cam-

erarius," or Chamberlain, which would give him the care of the dormitory, lavatory, and wardrobe of the community, and place him over the numerous officials and servants necessary to this office in so important and vast an establishment as Glastonbury then was.

Chapter III

Richard Whiting elected Abbot

In the month of February, 1525, Abbot Bere died, after worthily presiding over the monastery for more than thirty years. A few days after his death, on the nth of February, the monks in sacred orders, forty-seven in number, met in the chapter house to elect a successor. They were presided over by their Prior, Dom Henry Coliner, and on his proposition it was agreed that five days were to be left for consideration and discussion, and the final vote taken on the 16th. On that day, after a solemn mass de Spiritu Sancto the "great bell" of the monastery called the monks into chapter. There the proceedings were begun by the singing of the Veni Creator with its versicle and prayer, and then Dom Robert Clerk, the sacrist, read aloud the form of citation to all having a right to vote, followed by a roll call of the names of the monks. The book of the Holy Gospels was then carried round, and each in succession laid his hand on the sacred page, kissed it, and swore to make choice of him whom in conscience he thought most worthy. After this, one Mr. William Benet, acting as the canonical adviser of the community, read aloud the constitution of the general council Quia propter, and carefully explained the various methods of election to the brethren. Then the religious with one mind determined to proceed by the method called "compromise" (per formam compromissi), which placed the choice in the hands of some individual of note, and unanimously named Cardinal Wolsey to make choice of their abbot.

The following day the Prior wrote to the Cardinal of York, begging him to accept the charge. Having obtained the royal permission and after having allowed a fortnight to go by for inquiry and consideration, he, on March 3rd in his chapel at York Place, declared Richard Whiting the object of his choice. The Cardinals commission to acquaint the brethren of his election was handed to a deputation from the abbey consisting of Dom John of Glastonbury, the cellarer, and Dom John Benet, the sub-prior, and the document spoke in the highest terms of Whiting, He was described, for example, as "an upright and religious monk, a provident and discreet man, and a priest commendable for his life, virtues and learning." He had shown himself, it declared, "watchful and circumspect" in both spirituals and temporals, and had proved that he possessed ability and determination to uphold the rights of his monastery. This instrument, drawn up by a notary and signed by the Cardinal and three witnesses, one of whom was the blessed Thomas More, was handed to the two Glastonbury monks, who returned at once to their abbey.

They arrived there on the 8th of March, and met the

brethren in the chapter house, where they declared
the result of the Cardinal's deliberations. Then, at
once, Dom John of Taunton, the precentor, intoned
the Te Deum, and they wended their way, chant-
ing the hymn, from the chapter to the church, leading the newly elect. Meantime the news had spread
throughout the town. The people thronged into the
church to hear the proclamation, and as the procession of monks with Richard Whiting came from the
cloisters we can well picture the scene. The nave of
the mighty church was occupied by "a vast multitude" eager to do honour to him who was henceforth
to be their temporal and spiritual lord and father.
The glorious sanctuary of Avalon, enriched during
ten centuries by the generous gifts of pious benefac-
tors, had received new and costly adornments at the
hands of the abbot so lately gone to his reward. The
vaulting of the nave, which then rang with the voices
of the monks as they sang the hymn of praise, was
one of his latest works. The new-made openings in
the wall marked the places where stood King Ed-
gar's Chapel, and those of Our Lady of Loretto, and
the Sepulchre, more fitting monuments than was the
plain marble slab that marked his grave, of his love
and veneration for the ancient sanctuary of Glaston.
And as the monks grouped themselves within the
choir, the eye, looking through the screen which
ran athwart the great chancel arch – the porta coeli
– would have seen the glitter of the antependium of
solid silver gilt studded with jewels, with which the

same generous hand had adorned the high altar.

Into this noble sanctuary the people of Glaston crowded on that March morning in the year 1525 to hear what selection the great Cardinal had made. And as the voices of the monks died away with the last "Amen" to the prayer of thanksgiving to God for mercies to their House, a notary public, at the request of the Prior and his brethren, turned to the people, and from off the steps of the great altar proclaimed in English the due election of Brother Richard Whiting. Then, as the people streamed forth from the church bearing the news abroad, the monks returned to chapter for the completion of the required formalities. And first, the free consent of the elect himself had to be obtained, and he as yet remained unwilling to take up the burden of so high an office. He had betaken himself to the guest-house, called the "hostrye," and thither Dom William Walter and Dom John Winchcombe repaired, as deputed by the rest, to win him to consent. At first he determined to refuse, and then demanded time for thought and prayer; but a few hours after, "being," as he declared, "unwilling any longer to offer resistance to what appeared the will of God," he yielded to their solicitations and accepted the dignity and burden.

Then on Richard Whiting's acceptance being notified to the Cardinal, he sent two commissioners to

conduct the required canonical investigations into
the fitness of the elect for the office. On 25th March
these officials arrived at the monastery, and early on
the morning following, the Prior and monks came
in procession to the conventual church; in the presence of the Prior and convent they made a general
summons to all and any to communicate to them any
facts or circumstances which should debar Whiting from being confirmed as abbot; after this the
like obligation was laid in chapter on the monks.
Once more, at noon, the decree was published to a
"great multitude" in the church, and afterwards fixed
against the great doors.

Three days later, as no one had appeared to object
to the election, the procurator of the Abbot, Dom
John of Glastonbury, produced his witnesses as to
age and character. Amongst them was Sir Amyas
Paulet, of Hinton Saint George, who declared that
he had known the elect for eight-and-twenty years,
which was just the time when Henry VII had visited
Glastonbury, and Sir Amyas had been occupied in
extracting from the people of Somerset the fines levied for their real or supposed sympathy with Perkin
Warbeck and his Cornish rebels. The abbots witnesses testified that he had always borne the highest character, not only in Somerset, but elsewhere
beyond the limits of the diocese, and that none had
ever heard anything but good of him. One who so
testified was Dom Richard Beneall, who had been

a monk at Glastonbury for nineteen years, and who declared that during all those years Richard Whiting had been reputed a man of exemplary piety.

When this lengthy and strict scrutiny was finished the Cardinals commissioners declared the confirmation of the elect. Then, after the usual oath of obedience to the Bishop of the Diocese had been taken by the elect, he received the solemn blessing in his own great abbey church from Dr. William Gilbert, Abbot of Bruton and Bishop of Mayo in Ireland, at that time acting as suffragan to the Bishop of Bath and Wells.

In the pages of ecclesiastical history Wolsey's name meets with scant favour. Writers of all parties, whether they look on him with friendly or unfriendly eye, have little to say of his devotion to the best interests of the Church. Whatever his defects, due credit has not been given him for the real and enlightened care which he bestowed on the true welfare of the religious orders. For the Benedictines and Augustinians he designed, and in part carried out, measures of renovation, the fruits of which were already visible when Henry suppressed the monastic houses. It is evident that he was not content with general measures, but he fully acquainted himself with details and with persons. The election of Abbot Whiting is a case in point, and it is by no means improbable that the keen eye of the ecclesiastical statesman had marked him out at the general chapter of the Benedictines at Westminster, over which the great Cardinal had himself presided.

Thus was inaugurated the rule of the last abbot of Glastonbury, amid the applause and goodwill of all who knew him. Hitherto his life had been passed, as the life of a monk should be, in seclusion and unknown to the world at large. He had clearly not been one to seek for power or expect preferment, and his election to the abbacy of Glastonbury, though causing his name and fame to be spread wider, would after all, in the ordinary course of events, have given him in the main a local repute, and one of its nature destined, after life's day well spent in the peaceful government of his monastery, to pass into oblivion. Of course his position as head of one of the greatest of the Parliamentary abbeys (if the term may be used) obtained for him a place, and that no undistinguished one, in the roll of peers and in the House of Lords; and thus he would be brought naturally every year to the Court and the great deliberative assembly of the realm. But this was not a sphere which attracted a man of Whiting's temper and simple-minded religious spirit. His place was more fittingly found within his house, and in the neighbourhood which fell within the direct range of his special and highest duties. Here, then, he might have been best known and loved; and no further. But another lot was marked out for him in the designs of God. His life was to end in the winning of a favour greater than any which could be bestowed by an earthly power, for the crown of martyrdom was to be the reward of his devotion to daily duty. His fidelity to his state and trust issued in a final act of allegiance to Holy Church and to her earthly head which causes his name to be known and revered through all lands.

Chapter IV

Troubles in Church and State

The rule of Abbot Whiting over the vast establishment of Glastonbury had to be exercised in difficult times. Within a few months of his election Sir Thomas Boleyn was created Viscount Rochford, and this marked the first step in the king's illicit affection for the new peer's daughter, Anne, and the beginning of troubles in Church and State. For years of wavering counsels on the great matter of Henry's desired divorce from Katherine led in 1529 to the humiliation and fall of the hitherto all-powerful Cardinal of York.

Circumstances combined at this time to gather together in the social atmosphere elements fraught with grave danger to the Church in England. The long and deadly feud between the two "Roses" had swept away the pride and flower of the old families of England. The stability which the traditions and prudent counsels of an ancient nobility give the ship of State, was gone when it was most needed to enable it to weather the storm of revolutionary ideas. Most of the new peers created in the fifteenth and sixteenth centuries to take the place of the old nobles had little sympathy, either by birth or inclination, with the traditions of the past. Many were mere place-hunters, political adventurers, ready if not eager to profit by any disturbance of the social order. Self-interest prompted them to range themselves in the restless ranks of the party of innovation. Those who have nothing to lose are proverbially on the side of disorder and change. The "official," too, the special creation of the Tudor monarchs, was by nature unsettled and discontented, ever on the look-out for some lucky chance of supplementing an inadequate pay. Success in life depended, for men of this kind, on their attracting to themselves the notice of their royal master, which prompted them to compete one with the other in fulfilling his wishes and satisfying his whims.

At the head of all was Henry VIII, a king of unbridled desires, and one whose only code of right and wrong was founded, at least in the second half of his reign, on considerations of power to accomplish what he wished. What he could do was the measure of what he might lawfully attempt. Sir Thomas More, after he had himself retired from office, in his warning to the rising Crumwell, rightly gauged the king's character. "Mark, Crumwell," he said, "you are now entered the service of a most noble, wise and liberal prince; if you will follow my poor advice, you shall in your counsel given to His Grace, ever tell him what he ought to do, but not what he is able to do. For if a lion but knew his own strength, hard were it for any man to rule him."

Nor, unfortunately, were the clergy of the time generally fitted to cope with the forces of revolution, or hold back the rising tide of novelties. In the days when might was right and the force of arms the ruling power of the world, the occupation of peace, to which the clergy were bound, excited opposition from the party who saw their opportunity in a disturbance of the existing order. The bishops were, with some honourable exceptions, chosen by royal favour rather than for a spiritual qualification. However personally good they may have been, they were not ideal pastors of their flocks. Place-seeking, too, often kept many of the lords spiritual at court, that they might gain or maintain influence sufficient to support their claims to further preferment.

The occupation of bishops over much in the affairs of the nation, besides its evident effect on the state of clerical discipline, had another result. It created in the minds of the new nobility a jealous opposition to ecclesiastics and a readiness to humble the power of the Church by passing measures in restraint of its ancient liberties. The lay lords and hungry officials not unnaturally looked upon this employment of clerics in the intrigues of party politics and in the wiles and crafty business of foreign and domestic diplomacy as trenching upon their domain and as thus keeping them out of coveted preferment. Consequently, when occasion offered, no great difficulty was experienced in inducing them to turn against the clergy and thus enable Henry to carry out his policy of coercive legislation in their regard.

Five years after Abbot Whitings election to rule over Glastonbury the fall of Cardinal Wolsey opened the way for the advancement of Thomas Crumwell, who may be regarded as the chief political contriver of the change of religion in England. On the fall of the old order he built up his own fortune. For ten years England groaned beneath his rule – in truth it was a reign of terror unparalleled in the history of the country. To power he mounted and in power he was maintained by showing himself subservient to every whim of a monarch, the strength of whose passions was only equalled by the remorselessness and tenacity with which he pursued his aims. Crumwell fully understood before entering on his new service what its conditions were, and neither will nor ability was lacking to their fulfillment. Under his management, at once skillful and unscrupulous, Henry mastered the Parliament and paralyzed the action of Convocation, moulding them according to his royal will and pleasure.

Having determined that the great matter of his divorce from Katherine should be settled in his own favour, he conceived the expedient of throwing off the ecclesiastical authority of the pope* over the nation and constituting himself supreme head of the Church of England. Though the clergy struggled for a time against the royal determination, in the end they gave way; and on 3 November 1534, the "Act of Supremacy" was hurried through Parliament, and a second statute made it treason to deny this new royal prerogative.

The sequel is well known. The clergy caught in the cunningly-contrived snare of premunire, and betrayed by Cranmer, who, as Archbishop of Canterbury, had inherited Warham's office, but not his spirit, were at the kings mercy. With his hands upon their throats Henry demanded, what in the quarrel with Rome was at the time a retaliation upon the pope for his refusal to accede to the royal wishes, the acknowledgment of the king as supreme head of the Church of England. Few among English churchmen were found bold enough to resist this direct demand, or who even, perhaps, recognised how they were rejecting papal supremacy in matters spiritual. As a rule, the required oath of royal supremacy was apparently taken wherever it was tendered, and the abbots and monks of Colchester, of Glastonbury, and probably also of Reading, were no exception, and on 19 September 1534, Abbot Whiting and his community, fifty-one in number, attached their names to the required declaration.

It is easy, after this lapse of time, and in the light of subsequent events, to pass censure on such compliance; to wonder how throughout England the blessed

John Fisher and Thomas More, and the Observants, almost alone; should have been found from the beginning neither to hesitate nor waver. It is easy to make light of the shrinking of flesh and blood, easy to extol the palm of martyrdom. But it is not difficult, too, to see how reasons suggested themselves at least for temporising. To most men at that date the possibility of a final separation from Rome must have seemed incredible. They remembered Henry in his earlier years, when he was never so immersed in business or in pleasure that he did not hear three or even five masses a day; they did not know him as Wolsey or Crumwell, or as More or Fisher knew him; the project seemed a momentary aberration, under the influence of evil passion or evil counsellors, and it was on the king's part "but usurpation desiderated by flattery and adulation;" these counsellors removed, all would be well again. Henry had at bottom a zeal for the faith and would return by-and-bye to a better mind, a truer self, and would then come to terms with the pope. The idea of the headship was not absolutely new: it had in a measure been conceded some years before, without, so far as appears, exciting remonstrance from Rome. Beyond this, to many the oath of royal supremacy of the Church of England was never understood as derogatory to the see of Rome. While even those who had taken this oath were in many instances surprised that it should be construed into any such hostility.

However strained this temper of mind may appear to us at this time, it undoubtedly existed. One example may be here cited. Among the State Papers in the Record Office for the year 1539 is a long harangue on the execution of the three Benedictine abbots, in which the writer refers to such a view:

I cannot think the contrary [he writes], but the old bishop of London [Stokesley], when he was on live, used the pretty medicine that his fellow, friar Forest, was wont to use, and to work with an inward man and an outward man; that is to say, to speak one thing with their mouth and then another thing with their heart. Surely a very pretty medicine for popish hearts. But it worked madly for some of their parts. Gentle Hugh Cook [the abbot of Reading] by his own confession used not the self-same medicine that friar Forest used, but another much like unto it, which was this: what time as the spiritualty were sworn to take the king's grace for the supreme head, immediately next under God of this Church of England, Hugh Cook receiving the same oath added prettily in his own conscience these words following: "of the temporal church," saith he, "but not of the spiritual church."

Nor from another point of view is this want of appreciation as to the true foundation of the papal primacy a subject for unmixed astonishment. During the last half-century the popes had reigned in a court of unexampled splendour, but a splendour essentially mundane. It was a dazzling sight, but all this outward show made it difficult to recognise the divinely ordered spiritual prerogatives which are the enduring heritage of the successors of Saint Peter.

The words of Cardinal Manning on this point may be here quoted: "It must not be forgotten that at this time the minds of men had been so distracted by the great western schism, by the frequent subtraction of obedience, by the doubtful election of popes, and the simultaneous existence of two or even three claimants to the holy see, that the supreme pontifical authority had become a matter of academical discussion hinc inde. Nothing but such preludes could have instigated even Gerson to write on the thesis de auferabilitate Papa. This throws much light on the singular fact attested by Sir Thomas More in speaking to the jury and the judge by whom he was condemned, when the verdict of death was brought in against him: 'I have, by the grace of God, been always a Catholic, never out of communion with the Roman Pontiff; but I have heard it said at times that the authority of the Roman Pontiff was certainly lawful and to be respected, but still an authority derived from human law, and not standing upon a divine prescription. Then, when I observed that public affairs were so ordered that the sources of the power of the Roman Pontiff would necessarily be examined, I gave myself up to a most diligent examination of that question for the space of seven years, and found that the authority of the Roman Pontiff, which you rashly – I will not use stronger language – have set aside, is not only lawful, to be respected, and necessary, but also grounded on the divine law and prescription. That is my opinion; that is the belief in which by the grace of God, I shall die.'"

The lofty terms expressive of papal prerogatives might pass unquestioned in the schools and in common speech in the world, but from this there is a wide step to the apprehension, then none too common, of the living truths they express, and a yet further step to that intense personal realization which makes those truths dearer to a man than life.

To some, in Whiting's day, that realization came sooner, to some later. Some men, a few, seized at once the point at issue and its full import, and were ready with their answer without seeking or faltering. Others answered to the call at the third, or even the eleventh hour; the cause was the same, and so were the fate and the reward, though to the late comer the respite may perhaps have been only a prolongation of the agony.

It is of course impossible here to attempt even a sketch of the train of events which led to the destruction of Glastonbury and Abbot Whiting's martyrdom. The suppression of the monasteries has been

described as simply "an enormous scheme for fill-
ing the royal purse." As his guilty passion for Anne
Boleyn is the key to half of the extraordinary acts of
the succeeding years of Henry's reign, so is the need
of money to gratify his other appetites the key to the
rest. From the seizure of the first of the lesser religious houses to the fall of Glastonbury, the greatest
and most magnificent of them all, gain was the one
thought of the kings heart. To this end every engine
was devised, conscience was trodden under foot and
blood was spilled.

With the evident design of obtaining a pretext
for falling on the religious houses, the oath of supremacy in an amplified form was tendered to their
inmates. "There was presented to them," writes a
recent historian, "a far more severe and explicit
form of oath than that which More and Fisher had
refused, than that which the Houses of Parliament
and the secular clergy had consented to take. They
were required to swear, not only that the chaste and
holy marriage between Henry and Anne was just and
legitimate, and the, succession good in their off-
spring," but "also that they would ever hold the king
to be head of the Church of England, that the Bishop
of Rome, who in his bulls usurped the name of Pope
and arrogated to himself the primacy of the most
High Pontiff, had no more authority and jurisdiction
than other bishops of England or elsewhere in their
dioceses, and that they would for ever renounce the

laws, decrees and canons of the Bishop of Rome, if any of them should be found contrary to the law of God and Holy Scripture." This scheme failed, "for the oath was taken in almost every chapter-house where it was tendered."

Chapter V

Richard Whiting as Abbot of Glastonbury

The first years of Abbot Whiting's rule passed smoothly so far as the acts of his administration and his life at Glastonbury were concerned. He had of course to meet the troubles and trials incidental to a position such as was his. Moreover, for one who by his high office was called on to take a part, in some measure at least, in the great world of politics and public life, it could not be but that his soul must have been disturbed by anticipations of difficulties, even of dangers, in the not very distant future. Still, his own home was so far removed from the turmoils of the court and the ominous rumblings of the coming storm that he was able to rule it in peace. Discipline well maintained, a prudent and successful administration of temporals and kindly relations with his neighbours, high and low, were certain evidences that the government of Abbot Richard Whiting was happy and prosperous. Under such circumstances the position which he occupied as a peer of Parliament and as master of great estates was one which, as the world might say, even from its point of view, was eminently enviable.

It is somewhat difficult in these days to form a just and adequate idea of the place held in the country by one who filled the abbatial chair of Glastonbury.

For wealth and consideration, though not indeed for precedence, it may not unjustly be described as the most desirable ecclesiastical preferment in England. The revenues of the abbey exceeded those of the archbishopric of Canterbury itself, whilst, although the abbot had to maintain a large community and a great household, still he was exempt from the vast burdens necessarily entailed on so lofty a position as that of Primate of England, who was Legatus natusoi the Holy See and often a Cardinal. The annual value of the endowments of Westminster was, it is true, slightly greater, tut the ecclesiastical position of an abbot of that royal monastery was singularly diminished by the presence in his near neighbourhood of two such great churchmen as the Archbishop of Canterbury and the Bishop of London, whilst in its worldly aspect Westminster was overshadowed by the splendour of the regal court at its doors. Glastonbury in the sixteenth century had no rival in its own district; the day was past when the aspiring Church of Wells could raise pretensions on that score. In the west country there was neither prince nor prelate, certainly since the fall of the Duke of Buckingham, to compare in position, all considered, with the Abbot of Glastonbury.

But withal there existed in the court of the abbot, for his household was regulated like that of a court, a simplicity befitting the monastic profession. His own house was large, its rooms were stately, but it

did not pretend to the dimensions of a palace. He
had a body of gentry to wait upon him and grace the
hospitality he was ready to show to visitors the most
distinguished and to the poorer classes who thronged
the monastic guest-hall. To the great gate of the abbey, every Wednesday and Friday, the poor flocked
for relief in their necessities, and as many as five
hundred persons are said to have been entertained at
times at the abbot's table. Still, a combined simplicity and stateliness characterised the whole rule of
Abbot Whiting, and it is no wonder that, as we are
told, during his abbacy some three or four hundred
youths of gentle birth received their first training in
the abbot's quarters.

It may be asked by some how in such a position as
this, surrounded by all the world most ambitions,
Abbot Whiting could still be a monk. The position was not of his making; he found it. But that he
should ever remain a monk, that, as abbot, he should
be a true guardian of the souls committed to him, the
true father and pattern of his spiritual children, that
was by God's grace still in his power. That he was
all this, his very enemies have testified, and the explanation is simple. Raised to rule and command at
an age when, as he knew, the grave could not be far
distant, he was already a monk trained, disciplined,
perfected in outward habit and in the possession of
his soul by his long course of obedience. Tradition,
which is often so true in matters of small moment,

more than a century and a half after his death, still
pointed out among the ruins of his house, in the abbots simple chamber. Abbot Whiting's bed. It was
"without tester or post, was boarded at bottom, and
had a board nailed shelving at the head." This bed-
stead, according to the tradition of the place, was
the same that Abbot Whiting lay on, and "I was
desired," writes the visitor who describes it, "to observe it as a curiosity." The existence of the tradition
is proof at least of an abiding belief, on the spot, in
the simplicity of life of the last lord of that glorious
pile, the vast ruins of which were evidence of the
greatness of the monastery. It was possible even for
an Abbot of Glastonbury to preserve the true spirit
of poverty, and this was the secret of that excellent discipline which Dr. Layton to his bitter disap-
pointment found to exist at Glastonbury. The abbot
practised first what, as his duty imposed, he required
from those entrusted to his care, that is, from his
spiritual children, the monks of his house.

It was during these comparatively peaceful and
happy times that Leland, the antiquary, on his journey through England in search of antiquities, and
especially manuscripts, visited the abbey. He was
introduced to the library by Abbot Whiting in person, "a man truly upright and of spotless life and my
sincere friend" as he calls him. He was filled with
amazement at the treasures contained in the Glastonbury library. "No sooner did I pass the threshold,"

he writes, "than I was struck with awe and astonishment at the mere sight of so many remains of antiquity." He considered that the library had scarce any equal in all England, and spent some days in examining the shelves and the many wonderful manuscripts he found there.

With the conclusion of Henry's divorce case came the end of these peaceful years of Abbot Whiting's rule. Now began the anxious days which were to end for him in the death of the traitor, so far at least as the king's power could extend in death.

Within a year from the general oath-taking throughout England, and its failure to bring about the hoped-for result, Crumwell, ever fertile in expedients, had organised a general visitation of religious houses. The instruments he made choice of to conduct this scrutiny, and the methods they employed, leave no doubt that the real object was the destruction of the monasteries under the cloak of reformation. The injunctions are minute and exacting; in detail many were excellent; as a whole, even in the hands of persons sincerely desirous of maintaining discipline and observance, they were unworkable. In the hands of Crumwell's agents they were, as they were designed to be, intolerable. It was rightly calculated that under the pretence of restoring discipline they strike at the authority of religious superiors by the encouragement given to a system of tale-bearing. By other pro-

visions the monasteries were, with show of zeal for
religion, turned into prisons and reduced, if it were
possible, to such abodes of misery and unhappiness
as the uninformed Protestant imagination pictures
them to be. The moral of this treatment is summed
up by John ap-Rice and Thomas Legh, two of the
royal visitors, in a letter to Crumwell:

By this ye may see [they write] that they [the reli-
gious] shall not need to be put forth, but that they
will make instant suit themselves, so that their doing shall be imputed to themselves and no other.
Although I reckon it well done that all were out, yet
I think it were best that at their own suits they might
be dismissed to avoid calumniation and envy, and,
so compelling them to observe these injunctions
ye shall have them all to do shortly, and the people
shall know it the better that it cometh upon their suit,
if they be not discharged straight while we be here,
for then the people would say that we went for nothing else, even though the truth were contrary.

Armed with a commission to visit and enforce the
injunctions, Dr. Richard Layton, the most foul-
mouthed and foul-minded ribald of them all, as his
own letters testify, came to Glastonbury on Saturday,
21 August 1535. From Saint Augustine's, Bristol,
whither he departed on the following Monday, he
wrote to Crumwell a letter showing that even he,
chief among a crew who "could ask unmoved such

questions as no other human being could have imagined or known how to put, who could extract guilt from a stammer, a tremble or a blush, or even from indignant silence as surely as from open confession" – even Layton retired baffled from Glastonbury under the venerable Abbot Whiting's rule, though he covered his defeat with impudence unabashed. "At Bruton and Glastonbury," he explains, "there is nothing notable; the brethren be so straight kept that they cannot offend: but fain they would if they might, as they confess, and so the fault is not with them."

At this period it would seem that Richard Layton also spoke to the king in praise of Abbot Whiting. For this error of judgment, when some time later Crumwell had assured himself of the abbot's temper, he was forced to sue for pardon from both king and minister. "I must therefore," he writes, "now in this my necessity most humbly beseech your lordship to pardon me for that my folly then committed, as ye have done many times before, and of your goodness to instigate the king's highness majesty, in the premises."

Hardly had the royal inquisitor departed than it was found at Glastonbury, as elsewhere, that the injunctions were not merely impracticable, but subversive of the first principles of religious discipline. Abbot Whiting, like so many religious superiors at this time, petitioned for some mitigation. Nicholas Fitz-James, a neighbour, dispatched an earnest letter to Crumwell in support of the abbot's petition.

"I have spoken," he writes, "with my Lord Abbot of Glastonbury concerning such injunctions as were given him and his convent by your deputy at the last visitation there. . . To inform your mastership of the truth there be certain officers – brothers of the house – who have always been attendant on the abbot, as his chaplain, steward, cellarer, and one or two officers more, (who) if they should be bound to the first two articles, it should much disappoint the order of the house, which hath long been full honourable. Wherefore, if it may please your said good mastership to dispense the abbot, to dispense with the two first articles, in my mind you will do a very good deed, and I dare be surety he will dispense with none but with such as shall be necessary. . . . Other articles there are which they think very straight, howbeit they will sue to your good mastership for that at more leisure; and in the meantime I doubt not they will keep as good religion as any house of that order within this realm."

A month after this letter of Nicholas Fitz-James, Abbot Whiting himself ventured to present a grievance of another kind, affecting others than his community. The recent suspension by royal authority of the jurisdiction exercised by the abbey over the town of Glastonbury and its dependencies, had caused the gravest inconveniences. There are many "poor people," he writes, "who are waiting to have their causes tried," and he adds that he cannot believe that the king's pleasure has been rightly stated in Doctor Layton's orders. What the result of this application may have been does not appear, but it was clearly the royal purpose to let inconveniences be felt, not to remove them.

The proceedings taken in 1536 in regard to the suppression of the lesser monasteries must have filled the minds of men of Whiting's stamp with deep anxiety, as revealing more and more clearly the settled purpose of the king. "All the wealth of the world would not be enough to satisfy and content his ambition," writes Marillac, the French ambassador, to his master, Francis I. To enrich himself he would not hesitate to ruin all his subjects. The State papers of the period bear ample witness to the justice of this sweeping statement. The monasteries which were yet allowed to stand were drained of their resources by ever-increasing demands on the part of Henry and his creatures. Farm after farm, manor after manor was yielded up in compliance with requests that were in reality demands. Pensions in ever-increasing numbers were charged on monastic lands at the asking of those whom it was impossible to refuse.

Abbot Whiting was allowed no immunity from this

species of tyrannical oppression. The abbey, for instance, had of their own free will granted to blessed Sir Thomas More a comody or annuity. On his disgrace Crumwell urged the king's "pleasure and commandment" that this annuity should be transferred to himself under the convent seal. For a friend Crumwell asks (and for the king's vicegerent to ask was to receive) "the advocation of our parish church of Monketon, albeit that it was the first time that ever such a grant was made." A further request, for the living of Batcombe, Whiting was unable to comply with, since another of the king's creatures had been beforehand and secured the prize. In one instance an office which Crumwell had already asked for and obtained from the abbot, he a few months after demands for his friend "Mr. Maurice Berkeley;" and because the place was already gone, he requests that the abbot will in lieu thereof give the rents of "his farm at North wood Park." Abbot Whiting took an accurate view of the situation: "If you request it, I must grant it," he says; and adds, "I trust your servant will be content with the park itself, and ask no more."

The extant letters of Abbot Whiting, for the most part answers to such like applications for offices or benefices in his gift, are marked by a courteous consideration and a readiness to comply up to the utmost limits of the possible. It is, moreover, evident that he had an intimate concern in all the -details of

the complex administration of a monastery of such
extent and importance with its thousand interests,
no less than a determining personal influence on the
religious character of his community; and that public
calls were never allowed to come between him and
the primary and immediate duties of the abbot. He is
most at home in his own country, among his Somersetshire neighbours, and in the "straight" charge of
his spiritual children. Confident too in the affection
with which he was regarded by the population, he
had no scruples, whatever may have been his mind
in subscribing to the Supremacy declaration of 1534,
in securing for his monks and his townsfolk in his
own abbey church the preaching of a doctrine by no
means in accord with the royal theories and wishes
on the subject. Thus on a Sunday in the middle of
February, 1536, a friar called John Brynstan, preaching in the abbatial church at Glastonbury to the
people of the neighbourhood, said "he would be one
of them that should convert the new fangles and new
men, otherwise he would die in the quarrel."

By chance a glimpse is afforded of the popular feel-
ing in the district by a letter addressed to Crumwell
by one of his agents, always ready to spy upon their
neighbours and report them to their master, in the
hopes of gaining thereby the good graces of the
all-powerful minister. Thomas Clarke writes that
one John Tutton of Mere, next Glaston, – now by
the way safely lodged in gaol – had used seditious

words against the king and had spoken great slander against Crumwell himself. The depositions forwarded with this letter explain how Tutton had called one Poole a heretic for working on Saint Mark's day. Poole had replied that so the king had ordered, and upon this Tutton declared that they could not be bound to keep the king's command "if it was nought, as this was," and he added that "Lord Crumwell was a stark heretic." Nor did he stop here, for he continued in this strain; "Marry, many things be done by the king's Council which I reckon he knoweth little of, but that by such means he hath gathered great treasure together I wot well; there is a sort that ruleth the king of whom I trust to see a day when they shall have less authority than they have."

Knowing doubdess what would be the nature of its business, Abbot Whiting, excusing himself on the plea of age and ill-health, did not attend the parliament of 1539, which, so far as it could do, sealed the fate of the monasteries as yet unsuppressed. He awaited the end on his own ground and in the midst of his own people. He was still as solicitous about the smallest details of his care as if the glorious abbey were to last in avum. Thus an interesting account of Abbot Whiting at Glastonbury is given in an official examination regarding some debt, held a few years after the abbot's martyrdom. John Watts, "late monk and chaplain to the abbot," said that John Lyte, the supposed debtor, had paid the money "in

manner and form following. That is to say, he paid
£10 of the said £40 to the said abbot in the little
parlour upon the right hand within the great hall, the
Friday after New Year's Day before the said abbot
was attainted. The said payment was made in gold"
in presence of the witness and only one other: "for it
was immediately after the said abbot had dined, so
that the abbot's gentlemen and other servants were
in the hall at dinner." Also "upon Saint Peters day
at mid-summer, being a Sunday, in the garden of
the said abbot at Glastonbury, whilst high mass was
singing," the debtor "made payment" of the rest.
"And at that time the abbot asked of the said master
Lyte whether he would set up the said abbot's arms
in his new buildings that he had made. And the said
master Lyte answered the said abbot that he would;
and so at that time the said abbot gave unto the said
Mr. Lyte eight angels nobles. And at the payment of
the £30 there was in the garden at that time the Lord
Stourton. I suppose," continues the witness, "that
the said Lord Stourton saw not the payment made
to the abbot, for the abbot got him into an arbour
of bay in the said garden and there received his
money. And very glad he was at that time that it was
paid in gold for the short telling, as also he would
not, by his will, have it seen at that time." Thus too
almost the last glimpse afforded of the last Abbot of
Glastonbury in his time-honoured home shows him
in friendly converse with his near neighbour, Lord
Stourton, who was the head of an ancient race which

popular tradition had justly linked for centuries with
the Benedictine order, and which even in the darkest
days of modern English Catholicity proved itself a
firm and hereditary friend.

Before passing on to the closing acts of the venerable abbot's life and to his martyrdom, it is necessary to premise a few words on suppression in its
legal aspect. There seems to be abroad an impression
that the monasteries were all, in fact, dissolved by
order of Parliament, and accordingly that a refusal
of surrender to the king, such as is found at Glastonbury, was an act which, however morally justifiable
as a refusal to betray a trust, and even heroic when
resistance entailed the last penalty, was yet in defi-
ance of the law of the land. And, to take this particu-
lar case of Glastonbury, it is often stated, that when
insisting on its surrender the king was only requiring
that to be given up into his hands which Parliament
had already conferred on him. However common
the impression, it is false. What the act (27 Henry
VIII, cap. 28) of February, 1536, did was to give to
the king and his heirs such monasteries only as were
under the yearly value of £200, or such as should
within a "year next after the making of" the act "be
given or granted to his majesty by any abbot," etc.
So far, therefore, from handing over to the king the
property of all the monasteries. Parliament distinctly
recognised, at least in the case of all save the lesser
religious houses, the rights of their then owners, and

contemplated their passing to the king's hands only by the voluntary cession of the actual possessors. How any surrender was to be brought about was left to the king and Crumwell, and the minions on whose devices there is no need to dwell. Before a recalcitrant superior, who would yield neither to blandishments, bribery nor threats, the king, so far as the act would help him, was powerless.

For this case, however, provision was made, though but indirectly, in the act of April, 1539 (31 Henry VIII, cap. 13). This act, which included a retrospective clause covering the illegal suppression of the greater monasteries which had already passed into the king's hands, granted to Henry all monasteries, &c., which shall hereafter happen to be dissolved, suppressed, renounced, relinquished, forfeited, given up or come unto the king's highness. These terms seem wide enough, but there is also an ominous parenthesis referring to such other religious houses as "shall happen to come to the king's highness by attainder or attainders of treason." The clause did not find its way into the act unawares. It will be seen that it was Crumwell's care how and in whose case the clause should become operative. And with just so much of countenance as is thus given him by the act, with the king to back him, the monasteries of Glastonbury, Reading and Colchester, from which no surrender could be obtained, "were, against every principle of received law, held to fall by the attainder of their abbots for high treason."

The very existence of the clause is, moreover, evidence that by this time Crumwell knew that among the superiors of the few monasteries yet standing, there were men with whom, if the king was not to be baulked of his intent, the last conclusions would have to be tried. To him the necessity would have been paramount, by every means in his power, to sweep away what he rightly regarded as the strongholds of the papal power in the country, and to get rid of these "spies of the pope." Such unnatural enemies of their prince and gracious lord would fittingly be first singled out, that their fate might serve as a warning to other intending evil-doers. Perhaps, too, Whiting's repute for blamelessness of life, the discipline which he was known to maintain in his monastery and his great territorial influence may all have conduced to point him out as an eminently proper subject to proceed against, as tending to show the nation that where the crime of resistance to the king's will was concerned there could be no such thing as an extenuating circumstance, no consideration which would avail to mitigate the penalty.

Chapter VI

The Beginning of the End

In the story of what follows we are continually hampered by the singularly defective nature of the various records relating to the closing years of Crumwell's administration. We are therefore frequently left to supply links by conjectures, but conjectures in which, from the known facts and such documentary evidence as remains, there is sufficient assurance of being in the main correct.

Already, in 1538, rumour had spoken of the coming dissolution; and the fact that all over the country even the greatest houses of religion, one after another, were falling into the king's hands by surrender, voluntary or enforced, tended to give colour to the current tales. Henry's agents, it is true, had endeavoured to dissemble any royal intention of a general suppression of the monastic body. They not only denied boldly and unblushingly that the king had any such design, but urged upon Crumwell the advisability of putting a stop to the persistent reports on this subject. The far-seeing minister, fully alive to the danger, drafted a letter to reassure the religious superiors, and dispatched it probably in the first instance to Glastonbury.

"Albeit," this letter runs, "I doubt not but (having

not long since received the King's highness's letters wherein his majesty signified to you that using yourselves like his good and faithful subjects, his grace would not in any wise interrupt you in your state and kind of living; and that his pleasure therefore was that in case any man should declare anything to the contrary you should cause him to be apprehended and kept in sure custody till further knowledge of his grace's pleasure), you would so firmly repose yourself in the tenour of the said letters as no man's words, nor any voluntary surrender made by any governor or company of any religious house since that time, shall put you in any doubt or fear of suppression or change of your kind of life and policy." The king, however, feels that there are people who "upon any voluntary and frank surrender, would persuade and blow abroad a general and violent suppression;" and, because some houses have lately been surrendered, the king commands me to say "that unless there had been overtures made by the said houses that have resigned, his grace would never have received the same, and his majesty intendeth not in any wise to trouble you or to desire for the suppression of any house that standeth, except they shall either desire of themselves with one whole consent to resign and forsake the same, or else misuse themselves contrary to their allegiance." In this last case, the document concludes, they shall lose "more than their houses and possessions, that is the loss also of their lives." Wherefore take care of your

houses and beware of spoiling them, like some have
done "who imagined they were going to be dissolved."

This letter could scarcely have done much to reassure Abbot Whiting as to the king's real intentions,
in view of the obvious facts which each day made
them clearer. By the beginning of 1539, Glastonbury was the only religious house left standing in
the whole county of Somerset. Rumours must have
reached the abbey of the fall of Bath and Keynsham,
shortly after the Christmas of the previous year, and
of strange methods to which Crumwell's agents had
resorted in order to gain possession of Hinton Char-
terhouse and Benedictine Athelney. At the former,
the determination of the monks to hold to their house
was apparently in the end broken down by a resort
to a rigid examination of the religious on the dangerous royal-supremacy question, which resulted in one
of their number being put in prison for "affirming
the Bishop of Rome to be Vicar of Christ, and that
he ought to be taken for head of the church." This of
itself must have prepared the mind of Abbot Whiting
for the final issue which would have to be faced.

The short respite granted before conclusions were
tried with him, could have been to all at Glastonbury little less than a long-drawn suspense, during
which the abbot possessed his soul in peace, attending cheerfully to the daily calls of duty. They were

left in no doubt as to the real meaning of a dissolution and had witnessed the immediate results which followed upon it. The rude dismantling of churches and cloisters, the rapid sales of vestments and other effects, the pulling down of the lead from roofs and gutters, and the breaking up of bells had gone on all around them; whilst homeless monks and the poor who had from time immemorial found relief in their necessities at religious houses now swept away must have all crowded to Glastonbury during the last few months of its existence. For eleven weeks the royal wreckers, like a swarm of locusts, wandered over Somerset, "defacing, destroying and prostrating the churches, cloisters, belfreys, and other buildings of the late monasteries;" and the roads were worn with carts carrying away the lead melted from the roofs, barrels of broken bell-metal, and other plunder.

It was not till the autumn of the year 1539, that any final steps began to be taken with regard to Glastonbury and its venerable abbot. Among Crumwell's "remembrances," still extant in his own handwriting, of things to do, or matters to speak about to the king, in the beginning of September this year occurs the following: "Item, for proceeding against the abbots of Reading, Glaston and the other, in their own countries." From this it is clear that some time between the passing of the act giving to the crown the possession of all dissolved or surrendered monasteries, which came into force in April, 1539, and the

September of this year, these abbots must have been sounded, and it had been found that compliance in regard of a surrender was not to be expected. By the sixteenth of the latter month Crumwell's design had been communicated to his familiar Layton, and had elicited from him a reply in which he abjectly asks pardon for having praised the abbot at the time of the visitation. "The Abbot of Glastonbury," he adds, "appeareth neither then nor now to have known God, nor his prince, nor any part of a good Christian man's religion."

Three days later, on Friday, 19 September, the royal commissioners, Layton, Pollard and Moyle, suddenly arrived at Glastonbury about ten o'clock in the morning. The abbot had not been warned of their intended visit, and was then at his grange of Sharpham, about a mile from the monastery. Thither they hurried "without delay," and after telling him their purpose examined him at once "upon certain articles, and for that his answer was not then to our purpose," they say; "we advised him to call to his remembrance that which he had forgotten, and so declare the truth." Then they at once took him back to the abbey, and when night came on proceeded to search the abbot's papers and ransack his apartments "for letters and books, and found in his study, secretly laid, as well a written book of arguments against the divorce of the king's majesty and the lady dowager, which we take to be a great matter, as also divers pardons, copies of bulls, and the counterfeit life of Thomas Becket in print; but we could not," they write, "find any letter that was material."

Furnished, however, with these pieces of evidence as to the tendency of Whiting's mind, the inquisitors proceeded further to examine him concerning the "articles received from your lordship" (Crumwell). In his answers appeared, they considered, "his cankered and traitorous mind against the king's majesty and his succession." To these replies he signed his name, "and so with as fair words as" they could, "being but a very weak man and sickly," they forthwith sent him up to London to the Tower, that Crumwell might examine him for himself.

The rest of the letter is significant for the eventual purpose they knew their master would regard as of primary importance:

"As yet we have neither discharged servant nor monk; but now, the abbot being gone, we will, with as much celerity as we may, proceed to the dispatching of them. We have in money £300 and above; but the certainty of plate and other stuff there as yet we know not, for we have not had opportunity for the same; whereof we shall ascertain your lordship so shortly as we may. This is also to advertise your lordship that we have found a fair chalice of gold, and divers other parcels of plate, which the abbot had hid secretly from all such commissioners as have been there in times past; and as yet he knoweth not that we have found the same; whereby we think that he thought to make his hand by his untruth to his king's majesty."

A week later, on September 28th, they again write to Crumwell that they "have daily found and tried out both money and plate," hidden in secret places in the abbey, and conveyed for safety to the country. They could not tell him how much they had so far discovered, but it was sufficient, they thought, to have "begun a new abbey," and they concluded by asking what the king wished to have done in respect of the two monks who were the treasurers of the church, and the two lay clerks of the sacristy, who were chiefly to be held responsible in the matter.

On the 2nd October the inquisitors write again to their master to say that they have come to the knowledge of "divers and sundry treasons" committed by Abbot Whiting, "the certainty whereof shall appear unto your lordship in a book herein enclosed, with the accusers' names put to the same, which we think to be very high and rank treasons." The original letter, preserved in the Record Office, clearly shows by the creases in the soiled yellow paper that some small book or folded papers have been enclosed. Whatever it was, it is no longer forthcoming. Just at the critical moment we are again deprived, therefore,

of a most interesting and important source of information. In view, however, of the common sufferings
of these abbots, who were dealt with together, the
common fate which befell them, and the common
cause assigned by contemporary writers for their
death, viz., their attainder "of high treason for denying the king to be supreme head of the Church," as
Hall, the contemporary London lawyer (who reports
what must have been current in the capital), phrases
it – there can be no doubt that these depositions
were much of the same nature as those made against
Thomas Marshall, Abbot of Colchester, to which
subsequent reference will be made. It is certain that
with Abbot Whiting in the Tower and Crumwell's
commissioners engaged in "dispatching" the monks
"with as much celerity" as possible, Glastonbury
was already regarded as part of the royal possessions. Even before any condemnation the matter
is taken as settled, and on October the 24th, 1539,
Pollard handed over to the royal treasurer the riches
still left at the abbey as among the possessions of
"attainted persons and places."

Whilst Layton and his fellows were rummaging at
Glastonbury, Abbot Whiting was safely lodged in
the Tower of London. There he was subjected to
searching examinations. A note in Crumwell's own
hand, entered in his "remembrances," says:

"Item. Certain persons to be sent to the Tower for

the further examination of the Abbot of Glaston.''

At this time it was supposed that Parliament, which ought to have met on November 1st of this year, would be called upon to consider the charges against the abbot. At least Marillac, the French ambassador, who knows that he was always well informed on public matters writes to his master that this is to be done. Even when the assembly was delayed till the arrival of the king's new wife, Ann of Cleves, the ambassador repeats that the decision of Whitings case will now be put off. He adds that "they have found a manuscript in favour of queen Catherine, and against the marriage of queen Anne, who was afterwards beheaded," which is objected against the abbot. Poor Catherine had been at rest in her grave for four years, and her rival in the affections of Henry had died on the scaffold nearly as many years, before Layton and his fellow-inquisitors found the written book of arguments in Whitings study, and "took it to be a great matter" against him. It is hardly likely that, even if more loyal to Catherine's memory than there is any possible reason to suppose. Whiting would stick at a point where More and Fisher could yield, and would not have given his adhesion to the succession as settled by Parliament. But as in their case, it was the thorny questions which surrounded the divorce, the subject all perilous of "treason," which brought him at last, as it brought them first, to the scaffold.

It is more than strange that the ordinary procedure was not carried out in this case. According to civil law. Abbot Whiting and the Abbots of Reading and Colchester should have been arraigned before Parliament, as they were members of the House of Peers, but no such bill of attainder was ever presented, and in fact the execution had taken place before the Parliament came together.

The truth is, that Abbot Whiting and the others were condemned to death as the result of secret inquisitions in the Tower. Crumwell, acting as "prosecutor, judge and jury," had really arranged for their execution before they left their prison. What happened in the case of Abbot Whiting at Wells, and in that of Abbot Cook at Reading, was but a ghastly mockery of justice, enacted merely to cover the illegal and iniquitous proceedings which had condemned them untried. This Crumwell has written down with his own hand. He notes in his "remembrances":

Item. Councillors to give evidence against the abbot of Glaston, Richard Pollard, Lewis Forstell and Thomas Moyle. Item. To see that the evidence be well sorted and the indictments well drawn against the said abbots and their accomplices. Item. How the king's learned counsel shall be with me all this day, for the full conclusion of the indictments.

And then, to sum up all:

Item. The Abbot of Glaston to be tried at Glaston, and also executed there.

As Crumwell was so solicitous about the fate of the abbots as to devote the whole of one of his precious days to the final settlement of their case, in later times no less great was the solicitude of his panegyrist, Burnet, to "discover the impudence of Sanders" in saying they suffered for denying the king's supremacy, and to prove that they did not. Even at a time when records were not so accessible as they now are, Collier, Burnet's contemporary, could see clearly enough where lay the truth. "What the particulars were (of the abbots' attainder) our learned Church historian (Burnet) confesses he can't tell; for the record of their attainders is lost.' But, as he goes on, 'some of our own writers (Hall, Grafton) deserve a severe censure, who write it was for denying, etc., the king's supremacy. Whereas, if they had not undertaken to write the history without any information at all, they must have seen that the whole clergy, and especially the abbots, had over and over again acknowledged the king's supremacy.' But how does it appear our historians are mistaken? Has this gentleman seen the Abbot of Colchester's indictment or perused his record of attainder." He confesses no. How then is his censure 'made good? He offers no argument beyond conjecture. He concludes the Abbot of Colchester had formerly acknowledged the king's supremacy, and from thence infers he could not suffer now for denying it. But do not people's opinions alter sometimes, and conscience and courage improve? Did not Bishop Fisher and Cardinal Pool, at least as this author represents them, acknowledge the king's supremacy at first? And yet it is certain they afterwards showed themselves of another mind to a very remarkable degree. . . . Farther, does not himself 'tell us that many of the Carthusians were executed for their open denying the king's supremacy, and why then might not some of the abbots have the same belief and fortitude with others of their fraternity.'" (Eccesiastical History 2:173) The real way of reaching them was through conscience, a way which, as we have seen, had just before been tried in the case of the Abbot Whiting's near neighbours, the Carthusians of Hinton. "To reach the abbots, therefore," continues Collier," that other way, the oath of supremacy was offered them, and upon their refusal they were condemned for high treason. But amidst these cares Crumwell never forgot the king's business, the " great matter," the end which this iniquity was to compass. With the prize now fairly within his grasp, he notes:

The plate of Glastonbury, 11,000 ounces and over, besides golden. The furniture Of the house of Glaston. In ready money from Glaston,; 1,100 and over. The rich copes from Glaston. The whole year's revenue of Glaston. The debts of Glaston,; 2,000 and above.

Layton has borne witness to the state of spirituals in Glastonbury; Crumwell gives final testimony to the abbot's good administration of temporals. The house by this time had, according to Crumwell's construction, come to the king's highness by attainder of treason. It remained now to inaugurate the line of policy on which Elizabeth improved later, and after, in the secret tribunal of the Tower, condemning the abbot without trial for cause of conscience in a sentence that involved forfeiture of life and goods, to put him to death, so Lord Russell says, as if for common felony, the "robbing of Glastonbury Church."

And now it only remains to follow the venerable man on his pilgrimage to the scene of his martyrdom.

As we have seen under Crumwell's hand, Abbot Whiting's fate was already settled before he left the Tower. In the interrogatories, preliminary but decisive, which he had there undergone, the abbot had come face to face with the inevitable issue. He knew to what end the way through the Tower had, from the time of More and Fisher to his own hour, led those who had no other satisfaction to give the king' than that which he could offer.

It is not impossible, however, that hopes may have been held out to him that in his extreme old age and weakness of body he might be spared extremities; this supposition seems to receive some countenance from the narrative given below. But Henry and Crumwell had determined that Abbot Whiting should suffer before all the world the last indignity. And they designed for him the horrible death of a traitor in the sight of his own subjects who had known and loved him for many years, on the scene of his own former greatness.

The following extract from an unknown but contemporary writer, in giving the only details of the journey homeward that are known to exist, manifests the abbot's characteristic simplicity and perfect possession of soul in patience, together with a real sense of what the end would certainly be.

Going homewards to Glastonbury, the abbot had one Pollard appointed to wait upon him, who was an especial favourer of Crumwell, whom the abbot neither desired to accompany him, neither yet dared to refuse him. At the next bait, when the abbot went to wash, he desired Mr. Pollard to come wash with him, who by no means would be entreated thereunto. The abbot seeing such civility, mistrusted so much the more such courtesy was not void of some subtility, and said unto him: "Mr. Pollard, if you be to me a companion, I pray you wash with me and sit down; but if you be my keeper and I your prisoner, tell me plainly, that I may prepare my mind to go to another room better fitting my fortunes. And if you be neither, I shall be content to ride without your company." Whereupon Pollard protested that he did forbear to do what the abbot desired him only in respect of the reverence he bore his age and virtues, and that he was appointed by those in authority to bear him company of worship's sake, and therefore might not forsake him till he did see him safe at Glastonbury.

Notwithstanding all this, the abbot doubted somewhat, and told one (Thomas) Horne, whom he had brought up from a child, that he misdoubted (him) somewhat, Judas having betrayed his master. And yet though (Horne) were both privy and plotter of his master's fall, yet did he sweare most intolerably he knew of no harm towards him, neither should any be done to him as long as he was in his company; wishing besides that the devil might have him if he were otherwise than he told him. But before he came to Glastonbury, Horne forsook, and joined himself unto his enemies.

Chapter VII

The Martyrdom

The venerable abbot thus journeyed home in the
company of Pollard. It was this Pollard who had
been Crumwell's agent in sending him to the Tower,
who had weeks ago turned the monks out of the
monastery and had begun the wrecking of Glastonbury Abbey, a house, which on his first arrival there
he had described to his employer as "great, goodly
and so princely that we have not seen the like;" and
in another letter he repeats the same assurance, adding that "it is a house meet for the kings majesty, and
for no one else."

Measures had already been taken to have all secure
at Wells, although Abbot Whiting had evidently been
left in ignorance of the fact that there was now no
Glastonbury Abbey for him to return to. Crumwells
captive reached Wells on Friday, November 14, and
once safely brought back into his own country there
was neither delay nor dissembling. The plan devised
was rushed through without giving a soul among
the unhappy actors in the scene time to reflect upon
what they were doing – time to recover their better selves – time to avert the guilt which in some
measure must fall upon them. In accordance with
the wicked policy so often pursued in Tudor times,
a jury – the people themselves – were made active

agents in accomplishing the royal vengeance, the execution of which had been already irrevocably settled in London. John, Lord Russell, had for some time past been superintending the necessary arrangements in the county of Somerset itself. His business had been to get together a jury which he could trust to do, or perhaps in this case tacitly countenance, the king's will, and it was one part of his care, when all was over, to send to Crumwell their names with a view, doubtless, of securing their due . reward. Unfortunately, although Russell's letter is preserved the list enclosed has perished. But a letter from Pollard to Crumwell gives the names of some who distinguished themselves by their zeal, and who had been "very diligent to serve the king at this time." Among these first of all is "my brother Paulet," for whom is bespoken "the surveyorship of Glaston," with the promise to Crumwell that "his lordship's goodness," showed in this matter, Paulet when he takes the prize "shall recompense to his little power." Other diligent persons whom Pollard specially names are John Sydenham and Thomas Horner, and finally Nicholas Fitzjames, the same who, but a year or two before, had written to Crumwell in Abbot Whiting's behalf.

As is well known from the history of the Pilgrimage of Grace, jury-making had at this time been raised to an art, – an art so exquisitely refined that it aimed at making friends, kins-folk, even brothers the accomplices by word of mouth in the legal or illegal murders which disgraced this reign. The minds of the men selected in this case to register the decrees of the kingly omnipotence, escape our means of inquiry, but Lord Russell has recorded "that they formed as worshipful a jury as were found here these many years," and of this fact he "ensured" his "good lord" Crumwell.

Russell's care, moreover, had been diligently exercised, not merely in assembling the jury, but in getting together an audience for the occasion. His efforts were successful, for he gathered at Wells such a concourse of people, that he was able to declare "there was never seen in these parts so great appearance as were here at this present time." He adds the assurance so tediously common in documents of that pre-eminently courtly age, that none had ever been seen "better willing to serve the king."

This was the scene which met Abbot Whiting's eyes in Pollard's company as he entered the city of Wells, where so often before he had been received as a venerated and honoured guest. Unfortunately we have no direct and continuous narrative of all that took place. If it was dangerous to speak it was still more dangerous to write in those days, except of course in one sense, – that which was pleasing to the court. Fortunately two letters survive, written by the chief managers of the business, John, Lord Russell, and Richard Pollard, one of the "counsel" who had been engaged in the Tower with Crumwell, for the careful drawing of the indictment against the abbot. Both were written on the Sunday, the day following the execution. An earlier letter by Pollard, written on the day itself and evidently giving more details, is wanting in the vast mass of Crumwell's papers. This, the earliest news of the accomplishment of the king's will, was not improbably taken by the ready minister to the king himself and left with his majesty. Fragmentary though the records that exist are, and only giving here a hint, there a mere outline of what took place, without order and without sequence, they in this form have a freshness and truthfulness which still enable us to realise what actually took place.

On the abbot's arrival in the city of Wells, the business was begun without waiting to give the condemned man time for rest or for thought. Pollard was in charge of the indictment, over which Crumwell had spent his day, in the drafting of which so many counsel learned in the law had exercised their ingenuity, and which was the outcome of the secret examinations conducted during the abbot's two months' imprisonment in the Tower. But it was by no means intended that a drop of bitterness in the cup should be spared him; every successive stage of indignity was to be offered the venerable man till his last breath and then to his lifeless body. He was to be struck in the house of his friends, and by his own dependents. From out the crowd there came forward new accusers, "his tenants and others," putting up "many accusations for wrongs and injuries he had done them;" not of course that it was in the least intended that there should be time for enquiry into their truth; the mere accusations were enough, and they were part of the drama that had been elaborated with such care.

But this was not the only business of the day. The venerable man was to be associated and numbered with a rabble of common felons, and to stand in the same rank with them. Together with the abbot of the great monastery of Glastonbury there were a number of people of the lowest class – how many we know not – who were accused of "rape and burglary." "They were all condemned," says Russell, and four of them "the next day, if not the same day, put to execution at the place of the act done, which is called the Mere, and there adjudged to hang still in chains to the example of others."

Of any verdict or of any condemnation of the abbot and of his two monks nothing is said by Russell or Pollard, but they proceed at once to the execution.

It is not impossible, seeing the rapid way in which the whole business was carried through, that had the scene of the so-called trial been Glastonbury in place of Wells, the abbot would have met his fate and gained his crown that very day. But the king and his faithful minister, Crumwell, had devised in the town of Glastonbury a scene which was to be more impressive than that which had taken place in the neighbouring city, more calculated to strike terror into the hearts of the old man's friends and followers.

After being pestered by Pollard with "divers articles and interrogatories," the result of which was that he would accuse no man but himself, nor "confess no more gold nor silver, nor anything more than he did before you [Crumwell] in the Tower," the next morning, Saturday, November 15, the venerable abbot with his two monks, John Thorne and Roger James, were delivered over to the servants of Pollard for the performance of what more had to be done. Under this escort they were carried from Wells to Glastonbury. Arrived at the entrance of the town the abbot was made to dismount. And now all the brutal indignities and cruel sufferings attending the death of a traitor condemned for treason were inflicted upon him. And in truth, like many a true and noble Englishman of that day, Richard Whiting was, in the sense of Crumwell and Henry, a traitor to his king. The case from their point of view is well expressed by one of the truculent preachers patronised by the sovereign as his most fitting apologists.

"For had not Richard Whiting, that was Abbot of Glastonbury, trow ye, great cause, all things considered, to play so traitorous a part as he hath played, whom the king's highness made of a vile, beggarly, monkish merchant, governor and ruler of seven thousand marks by the year? Trow ye this was not a good pot of wine? Was not this a fair almose at one man's door? Such a gift had been worth grammercy to many a man. But Richard Whiting having always a more desirous eye to treason than to truth, careless, laid apart both God's goodness and the king's, and stuck hard by the Bishop of Rome and the Abbot of Reading in the quarrel of the Romish Church. Alas! What a stony heart had (Richard) Whiting, to be so unkind to so loving and beneficent a prince, and so false a traitor to Henry VIII, king of his native country, and so true, I say, to that cormorant of Rome."

In this new meaning of treason. Abbot Whiting was adjudged the traitor's death. At the outskirts of his own town his venerable limbs were extended on a hurdle, to which a horse was attached. In this way he was dragged on that bleak November morning along the rough hard ground through the streets of Glastonbury, of which he and his predecessors had so long been the loved and honoured lords and masters. It was thus among his own people that, now at the age of well nigh fourscore years, Abbot Whiting made his last pilgrimage through Enggland's "Roma Secunda." As a traitor for conscience sake he was drawn past the glorious monastery, now desolate and deserted, past the great church, that home of the saints and whilom sanctuary of this country's greatness, now devastated and desecrated, its relics of God's holy ones dispersed, its tombs of kings dishonoured, on further still to the summit of that hill which rises yet in the landscape in solitary and majestic greatness, the perpetual memorial of the deed now to be enacted. For, thanks to the tenacity with which the memory of "good Abbot Whiting" has been treasured by generations of the townsfolk, the very hill today is Abbot Whiting's monument.

His last act was simple. Now about to appear before a tribunal that was searching, just and merciful, he asks forgiveness first of God and then of man, even of those who had most offended against justice in his person and had not rested until they had brought him to the gallows amidst every incident that could add to such a death – ignominy and shame. The venerable abbot remains to the last the same as he always appears throughout his career; suffering in self-possession and patience the worst that man could inflict upon his mortal body, in the firm assurance that in all this he was but following in the footsteps of that Lord and Master in whose service from his youth upwards he had spent his life.

In this supreme moment his two monks, John Thorne and Roger James, the one a man of mature age and experience, the other not long professed, showed themselves worthy sons of so good a father. They, too, begged forgiveness of all and "took their death also very patiently." Even Pollard seems moved for the moment, for he adds with an unwonted touch of tenderness, "whose souls God pardon."

There is here no need to dwell on the butchery which followed, and to tell how the hardly lifeless body was cut down, divided into four parts and the head struck off. One quarter was despatched to Wells, another to Bath, a third to Ilchester, and the fourth to Bridgewater, whilst the venerable head was fixed over the great gateway of the abbey, a ghastly warning of the retribution which might and would fall on all, even the most powerful or the most holy, if they ventured to stand between the king and the accomplishment of his royal will.

All this might indeed strike terror into the people of the whole country, but not even the will of a Tudor monarch could prevent the people from forming their own judgment on the deed that had been done, and preserving, although robbed of the Catholic faith, the memory of the "good Abbot Whiting." It is easy to understand how, so soon after the event as Mary's reign, the inhabitants of the town and neighbourhood, with a vivid recollection of the past, were ready and even eager to make personal sacrifices for the restoration of the abbey. But even a hundred years later, and indeed even down to the present day, the name of Abbot Whiting has been preserved as a

household word at Glastonbury and in its neighbourhood. There are those living who, when convers-
ing with aged poor people, were touched to find the
affectionate reverence with which his name was still
treasured on the spot, though why he died and what
it was all about they could not tell. That he was a
good, a kind, a holy man they knew, for they had
been told so in the days of their youth by those who
had gone before.

Chapter VIII

Abbot Hugh Cook of Reading

The abbeys of Reading and Colchester, although of the first rank, seeing that their abbots were peers of Parliament, and Reading certainly among the most distinguished houses of the country, had no such position as that of Glastonbury. They were both Norman creations; Reading being founded by King Henry II and chosen by him as his burial place. By favour of its royal founder the commonalty of Reading recognised the abbot as their lord; the mayor of the city "being the abbot's mayor, etc.," as the diocesan, Bishop Shaxton writes, to Crumwell.

The history of the fall of Reading Abbey and of the execution of Hugh Cook, or Faringdon, the abbot, would be in its main features but a repetition of the story of Glastonbury and Abbot Whiting. The chief source of information about the Abbot of Reading is a paper, already referred to, which is still to be found among the public records, although it has remained unnoticed till four or five years ago.^ It was so decayed with age as to be almost dropping to pieces, but now encased in tissue paper it is fortunately legible almost in its entirety. The document in question is a virulent and brutal invective, evidently a sermon, drawn up for the approval of Crumwell, to be delivered in justification of the kings action in putting to death the three Benedictine abbots and their companions. It is unlikely that this proposed sermon was ever delivered, for the deed was done, the abbots were dead, their property was now all in the king's hands, and from the point of view of the authors the less said about the matter the better. The draft was accordingly thrown by Crumwell into the vast mass of papers of all sorts accumulating on his hands, which on his attainder was seized by the king and transferred, as it stood, to the royal archives.

It seems not improbable that the author of the paper in question was Latimer. The harangue is brutal; it shows all his power of effective alliteration, and it is written quite in the spirit of the man who begged to be allowed to preach at the martyrdom of Blessed John Forrest, and to be placed near him that he might with better effect insult him in his death agonies. It is certainly written by a person fully acquainted with all the circumstances, and throws light on many matters which would be unintelligible without it. The paper is so far of the highest value; but in dealing with its statements it is to be remembered that the one object of the writer is to blacken the memory of the martyred abbots, to degrade them and to bring them by every means into contempt.

From the account of Abbot Cooks origin given by this writer, it would be gathered that he was born in humble circumstances. He thus apostrophises the abbot after his death: "Ah, Hugh Cook, Hugh Cook, nay, Hugh Scullion rather I may him call that would be so unthankful to so merciful a prince, so unkind to so loving a king, and so traitorous to so true an emperor. The king's highness of his charity took Hugh Cook out his cankerous cloister and made him, being at that time the most vilest, the most untowardest and the most miserablest monk that was in the monastery of Reading, born to nought else but to an old pair of beggarly boots, and made him, I say, ruler and governor of three thousand marks by the year." But the testimony of the writer on a point of fact such as this cannot be rated high.

It is probable that Abbot Cook belonged to that class from which the English monastic houses had been so largely recruited, "the devouter and younger children of our nobility and gentry who here had their education and livelihood." There seems to be no doubt that he belonged to a Kentish family known to the heralds. His election to the office of abbot took place in 1520. Grafton and Hall in their chronicles, in accordance with the practice common at the time, to depreciate falsely by any and every means, those who had fallen into the disfavour of the reigning tyrant, give him the character of an illiterate person. "The contrary," writes Browne Willis, "will appear to such as will consult his Epistles to the University of Oxford, remaining in the register of that university, or shall have an opportunity of perusing a book entitled The art or craft of Rhetorick, written by Leonard Cox, schoolmaster of Reading. 'Twas printed in the year 1524, and is dedicated by the author to this abbot. He speaks very worthily and. honourably of Faringdon on account of his learning."

A letter written by Cook to the university in Oxford in 1530 is evidence of the abbot's intelligent zeal for the Catholic religion, which at that time was being attacked by the new heresies springing up on all sides. Among the monks of Reading abbey was one Dom John Holy man, "a most stout champion in his preachings and writings against the Lutherans," who, "desirous of a stricter life had resigned his fellowship at New College, Oxford, and taken the cowl at Reading Abbey." When Holy man was to receive the doctorate. Abbot Cook asked that he might be excused from lecturing before the university, as the custom was, so that he might preach in London, where there was greater need of such a man, seeing that the city was already infected with Lutheranism, and where the great popularity which Holyman already enjoyed brought crowds to hear him whenever he appeared in the pulpit at Saint Paul's.

On the visitation of Reading Abbey by Doctor London in 1535, the report was favourable as to the state of discipline. "They have," writes the Doctor, "a good lecture in Scripture daily read in their chapter-house both in English and Latin, to which is good

resort, and the abbot is at it himself." It is possible
that at this time in the visitors' injunctions as in their
report Reading was lightly treated. It must have been
known to them, as it evidently was to Crumwell, that
the abbot was in high favour with the king.

At any rate this circumstance will explain the sharp-
ness of a correspondence which took place at this
time between Shaxton, Bishop of Salisbury, in which
diocese Reading was situated, and Crumwell. The
latter takes up the very unusual position as defender
of an abbot, and administers a sharp reproof to the
bishop for his meddlesome interference in matters
in which, as Crumwell tells him plainly, he has no
concern beyond a desire to obtain preferment for an
unworthy dependent of his own.

It appears that the lecturer in scripture at the abbey
was one Dom Roger London, a monk of the house.
In the usual encouragement given to tale-bearing at
this time, some discontented religious had delated
their teacher to Bishop Shaxton as guilty of heresy.
"The matters were no trifles," says Shaxton, himself at that time a strong supporter of Lutheranism;
and the four points of suggested heresy certainly
run counter to the teaching of the German doctor.
Shaxton examined him personally, "as favourably
as I could do," he writes, "and found him a man of
very small knowledge and of worse judgment." In
the discussion which followed the bishop failed to

bring the monk to his mind, and this determined him to procure the appointment of a man after his own heart, one Richard Cobbes, who had been a priest and canon, but who was then "a married man and degraded." Shaxton applied to Crumwell for the appointment of Cobbes as lecturer to the monks in Dom Roger London's place "with stipend and commons" at the expense of the monastery.

Crumwell, on receipt of the bishop's letter, wrote to the abbot complaining that "the divinity lecture had not been read in the abbey as it ought to have been," and recommending Cobbes for the post of lecturer. Abbot Cook replied that he had already a fully qualified teacher, "a bachelor of divinity and brother of the house, who, by the judgment of others" better able to judge than himself, was "very learned in both divinity and humanities, profitting the brethren both in the Latin tongue and in Holy Scripture." He concludes by pointing out that this teacher read his lecture at far less charge than a stranger would do, and offers him to be examined by any whom Crumwell might appoint. As to the bishop's nominee, the abbot points out the condition of the man, and naturally declares him to be "a most dangerous man" to hold such a position in the monastery. Under these circumstances Abbot Cook refused to admit Cobbes into his house, and continued his monk, Dom Roger London, in the lectureship.

Finding that he had not got his way, Shaxton at once proceeded to inhibit the monk from reading at Reading, and put a stop to the lectures altogether. The bishop had evidently expected that Crumwell would out of hand have appointed Cobbes to the post on his first representation; "the which thing, if it had come to pass, so should I not have needed to have inhibited the said monk his reading; but I bare with him," he writes, "to say his creed, so long as there was hope to have another reader there. But when my expectation was frustrated in that behalf, then was I driven to do that which I was loathe to do and which, nevertheless, I was bound to do."

No one could have been more in sympathy with Shaxton's views on this matter than Crumwell. With the exception of the Archbishop of Canterbury and the Bishop of Worcester – that is, Cranmer, and Latimer – no one was more according to the ministers mind in religious matters than Bishop Shaxton; for all of them were true Lutherans at heart. Two of these prelates, indeed, continued honest in the year 1539 when brought face to face with the kings "Six Articles," which extinguished the immediate hopes of the Lutherans in England. They resigned their sees, whilst Cranmer, in accordance with his guiding principle, sacrificed his convictions and held to his archiepiscopal office.

In the matter of the Reading lectureship Shaxton

had counted that his ground was safe; and so indeed it was, up to the one point of that personal caprice which, throughout his reign, Henry maintained as the most cherished point of his royal prerogative. Whatever be the cause or explanation of the bishop's failure in this matter, one thing is clear: Henry had a real affection for the Abbot of Reading, so far as his affection could go, and used, as the contemporary libeller reports, to call him familiarly "his own abbot."

Shaxton was intent on doing his duty as a good pastor of sound Lutheran principles. But Crumwell had that all-determining and all-varying factor to consider, the kings fancy. He accordingly wrote to the abbot to tell him that he need not pay any attention to the Bishop of Salisbury's inhibition. "I," writes Shaxton on hearing of this, "could not obtain so much of you by word or writing to have your pleasure, and the Abbot of Reading could out of hand get and obtain your letters to hinder me in my right proceeding towards his just correction." Beyond this, not merely was the bishop's action set aside, but he had to submit to such a lecture from the king's vicar-general as may have decided him to resign his office when a few months later the "Six Articles" came to be imposed by the king and it was seen that the day for Lutheranism in England had not yet dawned. It will be sufficient here to quote the conclusion of Crumwell's letter, which dealt expressly with the matter in hand. "As for the Abbot of Reading and his monk," he writes, "if I find them as ye say they are, I will order them as I think good. Ye shall do well to do your duty; if you do so ye shall have no cause to mistrust my friendship. If ye do not, I can tell that (to) you, and that somewhat after the plainest sort. To take a controversy out of your hands into mine I do but mine office. You meddle further than your office will bear you, thus roughly to handle me for using of mine. If ye do so no more I let pass all that is past."

Whatever advantage the Abbot of Reading derived temporarily, at different conjunctures, from the king's partiality for him, it was by this time clear that such favour could be continued to a man of Abbot Cooks character only by the sacrifice of principles and convictions. According to the writer of the sermon already quoted, the abbot "could not abide" the preachers of the new-fangled doctrines then in vogue, and "called them heretics and knaves of the new learning." He was also "ever a great student and setter forth of Saint Benet's, Saint Francis', Saint Dominic's and Saint Augustine's rules, and said they were rules right holy and of great perfectness." It was, moreover, recognised that discipline was well maintained at Reading and Colchester no less than at Glastonbury; "these doughty deacons," as the writer calls the abbots and their monks, "thought it both heresy and treason to God to leave matins unsaid, to speak loud in the cloisters, and to eat eggs on the Friday." It would appear probable that Abbot Cook did not refuse to take the oath of royal supremacy, although there can be little doubt that in so doing he did not intend to separate himself from the traditional teaching of the Catholic Church on the question of papal authority. "He thought to shoot at the king's supremacy," as the contemporary witness has put it, and he was apparently charged with saying "that he would pray for the pope's holiness as long as he lived and would once a week say mass for him, trusting that by such good prayers the pope should rise again and have the king's highness with all the whole realm in subjection as he hath had in time past. And upon a bon voyage would call him pope as long as he lived."

After a page of abuse, the writer continues: "I cannot tell how this prayer will be allowed among Saint Benet's rules, but this I am certain and sure of, that it standeth flatly against our Master Christ's rule. . . . . What other thing should the abbot pray for here (as me-thinketh) but even first and foremost for the high dishonouring of Almighty God, for the confusion of our most dread sovereign lord, king Henry VIII., with his royal successors, and also for the utter destruction of this most noble realm of England. Well, I say no more, but I pray God heartily that the mass be not abused in the like sort of a great many more in England which bear as fair faces under their black cowls and bald crowns as ever did the abbot of Reading, or any of the other traitors. I wiss neither the abbat of Reading, the abbat of Glassenbury, nor the prior [sic] of Colchester, Dr. Holyman, nor Roger London, John Rugg, nor Bachelor Giles, blind Moore, nor Master Manchester, the warden of the friars; no, nor yet John Oynyon, the abbat's chief councillor, was able to prove with all their sophistical arguments that the mass was ordained for any such intent or purpose as the abbat of Reading used it."

"I fear me, Hugh Cook was master cook to a great many of that black guard (I mean black monks), and taught them to dress such gross dishes as he was always wont to dress, that he is to say, treason; but let them all take heed."

At the time of the great northern rising, the Abbey of Reading, together with those of Glastonbury and Colchester, is found on the list of contributors to the king's expenses in defeating the rebel forces. Reading itself appears to have had some communication with Robert Aske, for copies of a letter written by him, and apparently also his proclamation, were circulated in the town. Amongst others who were supposed to be privy to the intentions of the insurgent chief was John Eynon, a priest of the Church of Saint Giles, Reading, and a special friend of Abbot Cook, Three years later this priest was executed with

the abbot; but it is clear that at the time there was
not even a suggestion of any complicity in the insurrection on the part of the abbot, as he presided at
the examinations held in December, 1536, as to this
matter.

The first sign of any serious trouble appears about
the close of 1537. The kings proceedings, which
were distasteful to the nation at large, naturally gave
rise to much criticism and murmuring. Every overt
expression of disapprobation was eagerly watched
for and diligently inquired into by the royal officials.
The numerous records of examinations as to words
spoken in conversation or in sermons, evidence the
extreme care taken by the government to crush out
the first sparks of popular discontent. Rumours as
to the king's bad health, or, still more, reports as to
his death, were construed into indications of a trea-
sonable disposition. In December, 1537, a rumour
of this kind that Henry was dead reached Reading,
and Abbot Cook wrote to some of his neighbours to
tell them what was reported. This act was laid to his
charge, and Henry acquired a cheap reputation for
magnanimity and clemency by pardoning "his own
abbot" for what was, at the very worst, but a trifling
act of indiscretion.

The libeller thus treats the incident: "For think ye
that the Abbat of Reading deserved any less than
to be hanged, what time as he wrote letters of the

king's death unto divers gentlemen in Berkshire, considering in what a queasy case the realm stood in at that same season? For the insurrection that was in the north country was scarcely yet thoroughly quieted; thus began he to stir the coals a novo and to make a fresh roasting fire, and did enough, if God had not stretched forth His helping hand, to set the realm in as great an uproar as ever it was, and yet the king's majesty, of his royal clemency, forgave him. This had been enough to have made this traitor a true man if there had been any grace in him."

Circumstances had brought Abbot Cook into communication with both the other abbots, whose fate was subsequently linked with his own. In the triennial general chapters of the Benedictines, in parliament, in convocation they had frequently met; and when the more active measures of persecution devised by Crumwell made personal intercourse impossible, a trusty agent was found in the person of a blind harper named Moore, whose affliction and musical skill had brought him under the kindly notice of the king. This staunch friend of the papal party, whose blindness rendered his mission unsuspected, travelled about from one abbey to another, encouraging the imprisoned monks, bearing letters from house to house, and, doubtless, finding a safe way of sending off to Rome the letters which they had written to the pope and cardinals.

"But now amongst them all let us talk a word or two of William Moor, the blind harper. Who would have thought that he would have consented or concealed any treason against the king's majesty? Or who could have thought that he had had any power thereto? Who can muse or marvel enough to see a blind man for lack of sight to grope after treason? Oh! Moor, Moor, hast thou so great a delight and desire to play the traitor? Is this the mark that blind men trust to hit perchance? Hast thou not heard how the blind eateth many a fly? Couldst not thou beware and have kept thy mouth close together for fear of gnats? Hath God endued thee with the excellency of harping and with other good qualities, to put unto such a vile use? Couldst thou have passed the time with none other song but with the harping upon the string of treason? Couldst thou not have considered that the kings grace called thee from the wallet and the staff to the state of a gentleman? Wast thou also learned, and couldst thou not consider that the end of treason is eternal damnation? Couldst thou not be contented truly to serve thy sovereign lord king Henry VIII, whom thou before a great many oughtest and wast most bound truly to serve? Couldst not thou at least for all the benefits received at his grace's hand, bear towards him thy good will? Hadst thou nought else to do but to become a traitorous messenger between abbat and abbat? Had not the traitorous abbats picked out a pretty mad messenger of such a blind buzzard as thou art? Could I blazon thine arms sufficiently although I would say more than I have said? Could a man paint thee out in thy colours any otherwise than traitors ought to be painted? Shall I call thee William Moor, the blind harper? Nay, verily, thou shalt be called William Moor, the blind traitor. Now, surely, in my judgment, God did a gracious deed what time He put out both thine eyes, for what a traitor by all likelihood wouldst thou have been if God had lent thee thy sight, seeing thou wast so willing to grope blindfolded after treason! When thou becamest a traitorous messenger between the traitorous abbats, and when thou tookest in hand to lead traitors in the trade of treason, then was verified the sentence of our Master Christ, which sayeth. When the blind lead the blind both shall fall into the ditch. Thou wast blind in thine eyes, and they were blind in their consciences. Wherefore ye be all fallen into the ditch, that is to say, into the high displeasure of God and the king. I wiss, Moor, thou wrestest thine harpstrings clean out of tune, and settest thine harp a note too high when thou thoughtest to set the bawdy bishop of Rome above the king's majesty."

It is evident that in the Benedictine monasteries of the district as years went on there were many who, as they came to realise the true meaning of this new royal supremacy, made no attempt to dissemble their real opinions on the matter. The writer so frequently referred to thus expresses his conviction as to the attitude of the monks: "But like as of late by Gods purveyance a great part of their religious hoods be already meetly well ripped from their crafty coats, even so I hope the residue of the like religion shall in like sort not long remain unripped; for truly so long as they be let run at riot thus still in religion, they think verily that they may play the traitors by authority. But now his grace seeth well enough that all was not gold that glittered, neither all his true subjects that called him lord and master, namely, of Balaam's asses with the bald crowns. But I would now heartily wish," he adds, writing after the execution of the Abbots of Glastonbury, Colchester and Reading, "that as many as be of that traitorous religion [i.e., order] that those abbots were of, at the next' [assizes] may have their bald crowns as well shaven as theirs were."

On such suspicions as these the Abbot of Abingdon was called up to London and examined by Crumwell himself, whilst one of his monks was removed from the abbey to Bishop Shaxtons prison, evidently for his opinions on religious questions of the day, since he is designated by the Bishop as "the popish monk." Again one of Crumwell's spies reported his grave doubts as to Sir Thomas Eliot. It appears that Eliot had given out that he had himself told Crumwell that "the Imperator of Almayn never spoke of the Bishop of Rome but he raised his bonnet," and that he consorted in the country with " the vain-glorious Abbot of Eynesham," and with Dr. Holy man, evidently a relative of Dom John Holy man, the monk of Reading, and incumbent of "Hanborough, a mile of Eynesham," who is noted as "a base priest and privy fautor of the Bishop of Rome." Moreover, "he was marvellous familiar," so said the spy, "with the Abbot of Reading and Doctor London, Warden of New College, Oxon," a man, it is to be observed, in every way of different mind from his namesake. Dr. London, the royal visitor.

A letter from Eliot to Crumwell, in which he expresses his willingness to give up his popish books and strives to remove from the mind of the all-powerful vicar-general of the king the suspicion that he was "an advancer of the pompous authority of the Bishop of Rome," gives some insight into the nature of his communications with the suspected abbots. There "hath happened," he says, "no little contention betwixt me and such persons as ye have thought that I especially favoured, even as ye also did, for some laudable qualities which we supposed to be in them; but neither they could persuade me to approve that which both my faith and reason condemned, nor I could not dissuade them from the excusing of that which all the world abhorred. This obstinacy of both parts relented the great affection betwixt us and withdrew our familiarity."

In view of the prize to be won, that is, the broad acres and other possessions of the great monastic houses, any very definite enquiry as to the opinions of the inmates was not at once pressed home. Crumwell played a waiting game. The situation at Reading Abbey is well described by Dr. London, the visitor and royal agent in dissolving the religious houses, in a letter written to Crumwell whilst occupied in suppressing the Grey Friars' house in the town. "My lord," he writes of the abbot, "doubteth my being here very sore, yet I have not seen him since I came, nor been at his house, except yesterday to hear mass. The last time I was here he said, as they all do, that he was at the king's command, but loathe be they to come to any free surrender."

Still Crumwell evidently hesitated to try conclusions, and so matters remained for another year until he had obtained his Act of Parliament which provided for the case of a house "happening to come to the king's highness by attainder or attainders of treason." By the autumn of the year 1539 he was prepared for the final issue in the case of Reading. We have no records giving the details of Abbot Cook's arrest and his conveyance to the Tower. There is only the ominous entry in Crumwell's Remembrances early in September: "For proceeding against the abbots of Glaston, Reading and other in their countries." The Abbot of Reading seems to have been the first to be arrested, and there can be no doubt that they all remained for near two months in the Tower and were all subjected to the same enquiries. There is evidence to show that at Reading many arrests were made when the abbot was taken. A list of the prisoners in Tower on November 20th, 1539, includes the following, all connected with the abbey and town: Roger London, monk of Reading, Peter Lawrence, Warden of the Grey Friars at Reading, Giles Coventry, who was a friar of the same house, George Constantine, Richard Manchester and William Moor, "the blind harper;" and in one of Crumwells Remembrances at this time there is noted: "Item to proceed against the Abbots of Reading, Glaston, Rugg, Bachyler, London, the Grey Friars and Heron."

Abbot Cook, like the Abbot of Glastonbury, underwent examination and practical condemnation in the Tower before being sent down to his "country to be tried and executed." What was the head and chief of his offence we may take from the testimony of the hostile witness so freely used.

"It will make many beware to put their fingers in the fire any more," he says, "either for the honour of Peter and Paul or for the right of the Roman Church. No, not for the pardon of the pope himself, though he would grant more pardon than all the popes that ever were have granted. I think, verily, our mother holy Church of Rome hath not so great a jewel of her own darling Reynold Poole as she should have had of these abbats if they could have conveyed all things cleanly. Could not our English abbats be contented with English forked caps but must look after Romish cardinal hats also? Could they not be contented with the plain fashion of England but must counterfeit the crafty cardinality of Reynold Poole? Surely they should have worn their cardinal hats with as much shame as that papistical traitor, Reynold Poole. . . Could not our popish abbats beware of Reynold Poole, of that bottomless whirlpool, I say, which is never satiate of treason?"

Carried down to Reading for the mockery of justice, called a trial, the abbot and his companions could not swerve from their belief and their faith, but they maintained that this was not treason against the king. "When these traitors" says the libeller, "were arraigned at the bar, although they had confessed before and written it with their own hands that they had committed high treason against the king's majesty, yet they found all the means they could to go about to try themselves true men, which was impossible to bring to pass."

The writer's object was not to state the facts, but to cover the memory of the dead men with obliquy. Taking the document, however, as a whole, and bearing in mind the interpretation placed on the word treason at that time, there is no difficulty in penetrating into his meaning.

On November 15th, the same day upon which Abbot Whiting suffered at Glastonbury, the Abbot of Reading and two priests, John Eynon and John Rugg, were brought out to suffer the death of traitors. Here the same ghastly scene was enacted as at Glastonbury; the stretching on the hurdle, the dragging through the streets of the town. Abbot Cook, standing in the space before the gateway of his abbey, spoke to the people who in great numbers had gathered to witness the strange spectacle of the execution of a lord abbot of the great and powerful monastery of Reading. He told them of the cause for which he and his companions were to die, not fearing openly to profess that which Henry's laws made it treason to hold – fidelity to the see of Rome, which he went on to point out was but the common faith of those who had the best right to declare the true teaching of the English Church. "The Abbot of Reading, at the day of his death lamenting the miserable end that he was come unto," says our authority, perverting words and deeds to the greater glory of the king, "confessed before a great sight of people, and said that he might thank these four privy traitors before named of his sore fall, as who should say that those three bishops and the vicar of Croydon had committed no less treason than he had done. Now, good Lord for his Passion, who would have thought that these four holy men would have wrought in their lifetime such detestable treason?" And later on, speaking of the three abbots: "God caused, I say, not only their treason to be disclosed and come abroad in such a wonderful sort as never was heard of, which were too long to recite at this time, but also dead men's treason that long lay hidden under the ground; that is to say, the treason of the old bishop of Canterbury [Warham], the treason of the old bishop of Saint Asaph [Standish], the treason of the old vicar of Croydon, and the treason of the old bishop of London [Stokesley], which four traitors had concealed as much treason by their lives' time as any of these traitors that were put to death. There was never a barrel better herring to choose [among] them all, as it right well appeared by the Abbat of Reading's confession made at the day of [execution], who I daresay accused none of them for malice nor hatred. For the abbat as heartily loved those holy fathers as ever he loved any men in his life."

Thus, from the scaffold with the rope round his neck, and on the verge of eternity, the venerable abbot gave a witness to the veneration traditional in these islands from the earliest ages for the see of Rome, "in which the Apostles daily sit, and their blood shows forth without intermission the glory of God."

When the abbot had finished, John Eynon, the abbot's "chief counsellor," also spoke, evidently in the same sense, and begged the prayers of the bystanders for his soul, and the kings forgiveness if in aught he had offended.

This over, the sentence of hanging with its barbarous accessories was carried out upon Abbot Cook and the two priests, John Eynon and John Rugg.

The attainder of the abbot, according to the royal interpretation of the law, placed the Abbey of Reading and its lands and possessions at Henrys disposal. In fact, as in the case of Glastonbury, on the removal of the abbot to the Tower in September, 1539, before either trial or condemnation, the pillage of the abbey had been commenced. As early as September 8th Thomas Moyle wrote from Reading that he, "master Vachell and Mr. Dean of York" (Layton) had "been through the inventory of the plate, etc., at the residence" there. "In the house," he said, "there is a chamber hanged with three pieces of metely good tapestry. It will serve well for hanging a mean little chamber in the kings majesty's house." This is all they think worth keeping for the royal use. "There is also," the writer adds, "a chamber hung with six pieces of verdure with fountains, but it is old and at the ends of some of them very foul and greasy." He notes several beds with silk hangings, and in the church eight pieces of tapestry, "very goodly" but small, and concludes by saying that he and his fellows think that the sum of £200 a year "will serve for pensions for the monks."

On September 15th another commissioner, Richard Pollard, wrote from Reading that he had dispatched certain goods according to Crumwell's direction "and part of the stuff reserved for the king's majesty's use." "The whole house and church are," he says, "still undefaced," and "as for the plate, vestments, copes and hangings, which we have reserved" to the king's use, they are left in good custody and are to be at once conveyed to London. "Thanks be to God," he adds, "everything is well finished, and every man well contented, and giveth humble thanks to the kings grace."

Chapter IX

The Last Abbot of Colchester

The Abbot of Saint John's, Colchester, Thomas Marshall, writes Browne Willis, "was one of the three mitred parliamentary abbots that had courage enough to maintain his conscience and run the last extremity, being neither to be prevailed upon by bribery, terror or any dishonourable motives to come into a surrender, or subscribe to the king's supremacy; on which account, being attainted of high treason, he suffered death."

Thomas Marshall succeeded Abbot Barton in June, 1533, and entered upon the cares of office at a time when religious life was becoming almost impossible. At the outset he had apparently considerable difficulty in obtaining possession of the temporalities of his abbey. "I, with the whole consent of my brethren," he writes to Crumwell, "have sealed four several obligations for the payment of £200 to the king's use, trusting now by your especial favour to have restitution of my temporalities with all other things pertaining to the same. Unless I have your especial favour and aid in recovering such rents and dues as are withdrawn from the monastery of late, and I not able to recover them by the law, I cannot tell how I shall live in the world, saving my truth and promises."

Of the earlier career of Thomas Marshall little Is known except that he, like the majority of his order in England who were selected by their superiors for a university course, was sent to Oxford, where he resided for several years, and passed through the schools with credit to himself and his order. During this period he was probably an inmate of Saint Benedict's or Gloucester Hall, the largest of the three establishments which the Benedictines possessed in Oxford, and to which the younger religious of most of the English abbeys were sent to pursue their higher studies.

Very shortly after Abbot Marshall's election his troubles commenced. At Colchester, as elsewhere in the country at this period, there were to be found some only too anxious to win favour to themselves by carrying reports of the doings and sayings of their brethren to Crumwell or the king. In April, 1534, a monk of Saint John's complained of the "slanderous and presumptuous" sayings of the sub-prior, "D. John Francis." This latter monk, according to Crumwells informer, had "declared our sovereign lord the king and his most honourable council, on the occasion of a new book of articles, to be all heretics, whereas before he said they were but schismatics." These and other remarks were quite sufficient to have brought both the bold monk himself and his abbot into trouble at a time when the gossip of the fratry or shaving-house was picked up by eavesdroppers and carried to court to regale the ears of the Lord Privy Seal. In this case, however, the report came on the eve of the administration to the monks of Colchester of what was to be henceforth considered the touchstone of loyalty, the oath of supremacy. On the 7th of July, 1534, the oath was offered to the monks in the chapter house of Saint John's, and taken by Abbot Marshall and sixteen monks, including Dom John Francis, the sub-prior complained of to Crumwell.

Very little indeed is known about Colchester or the doings of the abbot from this time till his arrest in 1539. At the time of the northern rising, whilst the commissioners for gaol-delivery sat at Colchester, they were invited to dine at the abbey with the Abbot of Saint John's. When they were at dinner, as Crumwell's informant writes to him, one Marmaduke Nevill and others came into the hall "I asked him," says the writer, 'How do the traitors in the north?' 'No traitors, for if ye call us traitors we will call you heretics.'" Nevill then went on to say that the king had pardoned them, or they had not been at Colchester. They were, he declared, 30,000 well-horsed, and "I am sure," he said, "my lord abbot will make me good cheer;" and asked why, said, "Marry, for all the abbeys in England be beholden to us, for we have set up all the abbeys again in our country, and though it were never so late they sang mattins the same night." He added that in the north they were "plain fellows," and southern men, though they "thought as much, durst not utter it."

Another glimpse of the life led by the Abbot of Colchester during the few troubled years of his authority is afforded by a writer of a slightly subsequent period:

"Those who can call to mind the cruel deeds of Henry VIII, the confusion of things sacred and profane, and the slaughterings of which he was the author, will have no difficulty in recollecting the case of John Beche, Abbat of Colchester. Excelling many of the abbats of his day in devotion, piety and learning, the sad fate of the cardinal (Fisher) and the execution of Sir Thomas More oppressed him with grief and bitterness. For he had greatly loved them; and as he had honoured them when living, so now that they had so gladly suffered death for the Churches unity, he began to reverence and venerate them, and often and much did he utter to that effect, and made his friends partakers of his grief which the late events had caused him. And he was in the habit of extolling the piety, meekness, and innocence of the late martyrs to those guests whom he invited to his table, and who came to him of their own will, some of whom assented to his words, while others listened in silence. There came at length a traitorous guest, a violator of the sacred rights of hospitality, who by his words incited the abbat to talk about the execution of the cardinal and More, hoping to entrap him in his speech! Thereon the abbat, who could not be silent on such a theme spoke indeed in their praise but with moderation and sparingly, adding at last that he marvelled what cause of complaint the king could have found in men so virtuous and learned, and the greatest ornaments of Church and State, as to deem them unworthy of longer life, and to condemn them to a most cruel death. These words did this false friend carry away in his traitorous breast, to make them known in due season to the advisers of the king. What need of more? The abbat is led to the same tribunal which had condemned both Fisher and More, and there received the like sentence of death; yea, his punishment was the more cruel than theirs, for in his case no part of the sentence was remitted. Thus he was added as the third to the company of the two former. But why should I call him the third, and try to enumerate the English martyrs of that time, who are past counting? The writers of our annals mention many by name, but there were many more whose names they could not ascertain, whose number is known to God alone, for whose cause they died. Yet I hope that some day God will make known their names and the resting-places of their bodies, which were in life the dwelling-places of His Holy Spirit."

About the time of the arrest of the Abbots of Reading and Glastonbury, in September, 1539, reports were spread as to the approaching dissolution of Saint John's, Colchester. Sir Thomas Audley, the chancellor, endeavoured to avert what he thought would be an evil thing for the county. He had heard the rumours about the destruction of the two abbeys of Saint John's, Colchester, and Saint Osyth's, and, writing to Crumwell, he begs they may continue, "not, as they be, religious; but that the king's majesty of his goodness to translate them into colleges. For the which, as I said to you before, his grace may have of either of them £1,000, that is for both £2,000, and the gift of the deans and prebendaries at his own pleasure. The cause I move this is, first, I consider that Saint John's standeth in his grace's own town at Colchester, wherein dwell many poor people who have daily relief of the house. Another cause, both these houses be in the end of the shire of Essex, where little hospitality will be kept if these be dissolved. For as for Saint John's it lacketh water, and Saint Osyth's standeth in the marshes, not very wholesome, so that few of reputation, as I think, will keep continual houses in any of them unless it be a congregation as there is now. There are also twenty houses, great and small, dissolved in the shire of Essex already." Audley then goes on to protest that he only asks for the common good, and can get no advantage himself by the houses being allowed to continue, and concludes by offering Crumwell £200 for himself if he can persuade the king to grant his request.

The circumstances attending Abbot Marshall's arrest are unknown, but by the beginning of November, 1539, he was certainly in the Tower. On the 1st of that month Edmund Crowman, who had been his servant ever since he had been abbot, was under examination. All that was apparently extracted from this witness was that a year before the abbot had given him certain plate to take care of and "£40 in a coser."

The abbot's chaplain was also interrogated as to any words he had heard the abbot speak against the king at any time, but little information was elicited from him. The most important piece of evidence is a document, which, as it contains declarations as to Abbot Marshall's opinions upon several important matters, and as it is almost the only record of the examinations of witnesses against any of the three abbots, and gives a sample of the questions on which all these examinations in the Tower concerning treason must have turned, may here be given as nearly as possible in the original form.

Interrogatories ministered unto Robert Rowse, mercer, of Colchester, 4 Novembris anno regni Henrici octavi tricesimo primo (1539). Ad primam, the said Rowse sworne upon the Evangel, and sayeth that he hath known the Abbat of Colchester the space of six years at midsummer last past or thereabout, about which time the said was elected abbat. And within a

sennight after or thereabout this examinant sent unto
the said abbat a dish of bass (baces) and a bottle of
wine to the welcome. Upon the which present the
said abbat did send for the examinant to dine with
him upon a Friday, at which time they were first acquainted, and since was divers times in his company
and familiar with him unto a fortnight before the
feast of All Hallows was two years past. – Robert
Rowse.

2. Ad secundam, he sayeth that the principal cause
why that he did leave the company of the said abbat
was because that abbat was divers times commun-
ing and respuing against the king's majesty's supremacy and such ordinances as were passed by the
act of Parliament concerning the extinguishment of
the bishop of Rome's usurped authority, saying that
the whole authority was given by Christ unto Peter and to his successors, bishops of Rome, to bind
and to loose, and to grant pardons for sin, and to be
chief and supreme head of the Church throughout
all Christian realms immediate and next unto Christ,
and that it was against God's commandment and His
laws that any temporal prince should be head of the
Church. And also he said that the king's highness
had evil counsel that moved him to take on hand to
be chief head of the Church of England and to pull
down these houses of religion which were founded
by his grace's progenitors and many noble men for
the service and honour of God, the commonwealth,

and relief of poor folk, and that the same was both against God's law and man's law; and furthermore, he said that by means of the premises the king and his council were drawn into such an inordinate covetousness that if all the water in the Thames were flowing gold and silver it were not able to slake their covetousness, and said a vengeance of all such councillors. – Robert Rowse.

3. Ad tertiam, he sayeth that he is not well remembered of the year nor of the days that the said abbat had the foresaid communications because he spoke at divers times, and specially at such times as he heard that any such matters were had in use, and furthermore of this he is well remembered of that at such time as the monks of Syon, the Bishop of Rochester, and Sir Thomas More were put to execution, the said abbat would say that he marvelled greatly of such tyranny as was used by the king and his council to put such holy men to death, and further the abbat said that in his opinion they died holy martyrs and in the right of Christ's Church. – Robert Rowse.

4. Ad quartam, he sayeth that the last time that ever he heard the said abbat have any communication of such matters was, immediately after that he heard of the insurrection in the north parts, he sent for this examinant to come to sup with him, and in the mean time that supper was making ready the abbat

and the examinant were walking between the hall
and the garden in a little gallery off the ground, and
then and there the abbat asked of this examinant
what news he heard of the coast? And this examinant said that he heard none. Then the abbat said:
"Dost you not hear of the insurrection in the north?"
And this examinant said "no." "The northern lads be
up and they begin to take pip in the webe [sic] and
say plainly that they will have no more abbeys suppressed in their country; " and he said to this examinant that the northern men were as true subjects unto
the king as anywhere within his realm, and that they
desired nothing of the king but that they might have
delivered unto their hands the Archbishop of Canterbury, the lord chancellor, and the lord privy seal; and
the abbat said "would to God that the northern men
had them, for then (he said) we should have a merry
world, for they were three arch-heretics," which
term this examinant never heard before; and so then
they went to supper, and since this time, which was
as this examinant doth remember a fortnight or three
weeks before the feast of All Saints, was two years.
– Robert Rowse.

The evidence of Thomas Nuthake, a "physition," of
Colchester, is to the like effect. He had not, he said,
to his knowledge seen or known Abbot Thomas
before his election, although he had divers times
repaired to the abbey before that time. In reply to the
third question, this doctor "sayeth that concerning

the marriage of queen Anne this examinant remembers he hath heard the said abbat say that the reason why the kings highness did forsake the bishop of Rome was to the intent that his majesty might be divorced from the lady dowager and wed queen Anne, and therefore his grace refused to take the bishop of Rome for the supreme head of the Church, and made himself the supreme head."

Another of the witnesses against the Lord Abbot of Colchester was a cleric, John Seyn, who deposed that when he had informed him of his neighbour, the Abbot of Saint Osyth's surrender of his monastery to the king, he answered, "I will not say the king shall never have my house, but it will be against my will and against my heart, for I know by my learning that he cannot take it by right and law, wherefore in my conscience I cannot be content, nor he shall never have it with my heart and will." Whereunto John Seyn, clerk, answered in this wise: " Beware of such learning as ye learned at Oxenford when ye were young. Ye would be hanged and ye are worthy. I will advise you to conform yourself as a true subject, or else you shall hinder your brethren and also yourself."

Nothing more is known of Abbot Marshall's last days, but the fact of his execution as a traitor on 1 December 1539. The enamelled pectoral cross of the venerable martyr has been preserved, and is now in possession of the Lord Clifford of Chudleigh. On one side it bears the emblems of the Five Wounds, in the centre the Sacred Heart of our Lord, surrounded by the crown of thorns, above which is the inscription, "I.N.R.I.," and below it the sacred monogram, "I.H.S." with the wounded hands and feet of our Saviour. On the back the instruments of the Passion are engraved. The following inscriptions in Latin appear in and about the cross: "May the Passion of our Lord Jesus Christ bring us out of sorrow and sadness. This sign of the cross shall be in the heavens when our Lord shall come to judgment. Behold, O man! Thy Redeemer suffers for thee. He who will come after me, let him take up his cross and follow me."

It is curious to observe how frequently in this world malice defeats its own ends even when it takes a guise, to some persons apparently so attractive, of doing God a service. It is by a singular fate that the would-be preacher, who gave himself so much trouble to defame the three Abbots of Glastonbury, Reading and Colchester and their companions, in the expectation doubtless of thereby recommending him- self to the king, should have been, after three centuries and a half of oblivion, the most explicit witness of the cause for which these venerable men gave up their lives in all the terrors of as shameful and painful a death as man could devise.

The writer himself amid the periods which betoken his unhappy spirit, seems to have been haunted still with some forebodings that he was destined to make manifest a truth which it was the evident design of those in power to shroud in obscurity. He cannot help being truculent even at his best; but the form which he adopts may well be pardoned for the sake of the sense. "Is it not to be thought, trow ye," he says, "that forasmuch as these trusty traitors have so valiantly jeopardied a joint for the Bishop of Rome's sake, that his Holiness will after their hanging canvass them, canonise them, I would say, for their labours and pains. It is not to be doubted but his Holiness will look upon their pains as upon Thomas Becket's, seeing it is for like matter."

Much has since happened which the writer of these words could not have anticipated. In God's hands are times and seasons, and He alone it is Who judges rightly the acts and lives of men. The words of the wise man fittingly rise up in the mind as it recalls the story of the deaths of these holy abbots. "In the sight of the unwise they seemed to die: and their departure was taken for misery, and their going away from us for utter destruction: but they are in peace. And though in the sight of men they suffered torments, their hope is full of immortality. Afflicted in few things, in many they shall be well rewarded; because God has tried them and found them worthy of Himself. As gold in the furnace He hath proved them, and as a victim of a holocaust He hath received them, and in time there shall be respect had unto them."